THE WRIGHT
BROTHERS

Aviation Pioneers and Inventors

Wendie C. Old

Enslow Publishers, Inc.
40 Industrial Road
Box 398
Berkeley Heights, NJ 07922
USA

http://www.enslow.com

Originally published as *The Wright Brothers: Inventors of the Airplane* in 2000.

No part of this book may be reproduced by any means
without the written permission of the publisher.

Library of Congress Cataloging-in-Publication Data

Old, Wendie C., author..
    The Wright brothers : aviation pioneers and inventors / Wendie C. Old.
        pages cm. — (Legendary American biographies)
    "Originally published as: The Wright Brothers: Inventors of the Airplane in 2000."
    Summary: "Traces the path of the Wright Brothers as they pursued their dream of
changing the world of aviation."— Provided by publisher.
    Audience: Grades 4 to 6.
    Includes bibliographical references and index.
    ISBN 978-0-7660-6505-5 (hardcover)
    1. Wright, Orville, 1871–1948—Juvenile literature. 2. Wright, Wilbur, 1867–
1912—Juvenile literature. 3. Inventors—United States—Biography—Juvenile
literature. 4. Aeronautics—United States—Biography—Juvenile literature. I. Title.
    TL540.W7O43 2015
    629.13'0092'2—dc23

                  2014029271

Future Editions:
Paperback ISBN: 978-0-7660-6506-2
EPUB ISBN: 978-0-7660-6507-9
Single-User PDF ISBN: 978-0-7660-6508-6
Multi-User PDF ISBN: 978-0-7660-6509-3

Printed in the United States of America

102014 Bang Printing, Brainerd, Minn.

10 9 8 7 6 5 4 3 2 1

To Our Readers: We have done our best to make sure all Internet addresses in this book
were active and appropriate when we went to press. However, the author and the publisher
have no control over and assume no liability for the material available on those Internet sites
or on other Web sites they may link to. Send comments to comments@enslow.com or to the
address on the back cover.

✪ Enslow Publishers, Inc., is committed to printing our books on recycled paper. The paper
in every book contains 10% to 30% post-consumer waste (PCW). The cover board on the
outside of each book contains 100% PCW. Our goal is to do our part to help young people
and the environment too!

Illustration Credits: Library of Congress, pp. 4, 6, 10, 20, 32, 37, 48; Shutterstock.com:
© A-R-T (scrolls).

Cover Illustration: Library of Congress

CONTENTS

Wilbur(left) and Orville Wright are still remembered for their amazing accomplishments and for starting the age of aviation.

Chapter 1

SUCCESS

S ince the early 1980s, 6 million license plates have told the world that North Carolina is "First in Flight."[1] Why? Because two bicycle builders from Dayton, Ohio, used the Outer Banks of North Carolina for their research about flight. They needed the barren sand dunes, the open spaces, and the constant seashore wind to test their experimental craft.

Wilbur and Orville Wright came yearly to the lonely windswept area from 1900 to 1903. There, they tested gliders at the large sand dunes, called Kill Devil Hills, four miles south of the small village of Kitty Hawk.

In the fall of 1903, their double-winged, motor-propelled contraption—named the Flyer—was ready to be tested with a man aboard. To lift their Flyer into the air, the Wright brothers calculated that they would need a lightweight motor that produced at least nine horsepower.

None of the newly invented automobile companies could supply a motor that exactly suited the needs of the Wright brothers. The brothers had to build their own motor out of cast aluminum and steel. They used aluminum because it is a strong as well as a lightweight metal.

According to their calculations, their motor would produce the needed nine horsepower. To their surprise, it actually generated twelve horsepower—more than enough to lift the Flyer into the air.

The Flyer was partially constructed in Dayton and weighed before shipping to Kitty Hawk, North Carolina. In the end, the Wrights calculated its weight to be 675 pounds. Although slightly heavier than the Wrights had wanted, they thought it still might lift off the ground with the stronger horsepower engine.

Rear view of the Wright brothers' four-cylinder motor as installed in their 1903 airplane. Orville and Wilbur designed the engine used in the first successful flight. Charlie Taylor built the engine under their direction.

On the Outer Banks

More storms hit the Outer Banks during the fall of 1903 than in previous years. Between the storms, the Wright brothers pieced together the Flyer in the wooden shed at their camp near Kill Devil Hills.

However, the first test of the engine on November 5 damaged the propeller shafts. These had to be sent to the mainland to be repaired. When they were reinstalled, the brothers spent a week adjusting them. On November 28, one of the propeller shafts cracked. Orville took it home to Dayton to be repaired.

While Wilbur waited for Orville to return, the weather became mild and clear. The next week was perfect flying weather. In fact, several hundred miles north, another aviator was preparing to prove that his airplane design would be the first to fly.

The Competition

Samuel Pierpont Langley, the head of the Smithsonian Institution in Washington, D.C., had experimented with flight for years. He was a trained scientist, and his work was supported by government money. He planned to launch his Great Aerodrome over water.

On Tuesday, December 8, tugboats pulled a large houseboat from a wharf at the foot of Eighth Street in southwest Washington, D.C. They plowed through patches of floating ice to the junction of the Potomac and Anacosta rivers.

Langley had run out of money. This was his last chance. He watched from shore with a small party of friends, including Alexander Graham Bell, inventor of the telephone, and some Smithsonian employees. The pilot, Charles Manly, stripped off his outer clothing. To cut down on weight, he would fly in his long underwear and a cork-lined life jacket.

At 4:45 P.M., the Great Aerodrome was thrown off the houseboat by a catapult. It slid along a track. When it reached the edge of the roof of the houseboat, instead of flying, Manly felt a sharp jerk. He did not see water below him. He saw sky. The

Aerodrome had flipped over. Its wings were shaped wrong. They could not lift the Great Aerodrome into the sky. Instead, it splashed into the water.

Manly became tangled in the broken wood and wire under water. As he tried to surface, he encountered ice above his head. Finally, he reached open water and was pulled out of the freezing river.

Langley's twenty-year struggle to fly had failed. The newspapers made fun of him. Another foolish person had fought the law of gravity and had lost.

The Wrights' First Attempt

Meanwhile, Orville Wright returned to the Outer Banks with the repaired propeller shaft. On December 14, members of the nearby Kill Devil Hills Lifesaver Corps helped the Wrights drag the Flyer to the base of a nearby dune and lay a single rail. The brothers' first attempt at flying would use a nine-degree slope down the dune to get a gravity-assisted start.

While the engine putted away, the brothers tossed a coin. Who would have the honor of the world's first power-assisted manned flight? Wilbur, the older brother, won the toss.

Wilbur jumped into the Flyer at the top of the track. He lay on the lower wing. He tested to make sure all the controls were within reach. They worked. Suddenly, the Flyer was moving!

Orville ran alongside the right wingtip to help steady the craft. Forty feet along, it flew out of his hands. The Flyer was flying—pushed by propellers and steered by Wilbur. However, it was not under control. It nosed up about fifteen feet into the air, then stalled. Sixty feet from the end of the rail it dove for the sand and crashed.

The left wingtip caught in the sand. The Flyer swung around. The front skids hit the sand, splintering a front elevator support. The sudden crashing stop stunned Wilbur. Eventually, he reached

Taking Off From the Ground

To guide the takeoff, the men built a sixty-foot takeoff rail. This single rail was made up of a series of wooden two-by-fours set in the sand on edge. The upper edge of the rail was protected by a thin strip of metal. Bicycle wheels (without tires) were attached to a length of wood that supported the Flyer's skids and guided the craft straight along the monorail. There were no wheels on the plane itself. Those came much later. For several years, the Wright brothers used skids or runners, like those on snow sleds, on their Flyers.

up and switched the engine off. Their first attempt at controlled, heavier-than-air, manned flight had failed.

Orville sent a telegraph message to their family in Dayton. "Misjudgment at start . . . success assured keep quiet."[2] He did not want the newspapers to make fun of their attempts, as they had with Langley and other experimenters.

The First Flight

It took two days to repair the Flyer. On the third day, the winds died down and they could not fly. December 17 dawned with a cold, twenty-four-mile-per-hour wind. Frozen puddles of water sparkled in the sand. The brothers discussed whether they should wait for warmer weather with more moderate wind. If they waited too long, they might not make it home for Christmas.

They decided to go ahead. A flag signaled the men at the Kill Devil Hills Lifesaving Station to come help with the flight. Three men responded. They were John T. Daniels, W. S. Dough, and A. D. Etheridge. W. D. Brinkley, a lumber buyer, and Johnny Moore, a curious boy from nearby Nags Head, also followed the men.

After many attempts, the Wright brothers were successful as the Flyer lifted off the guide rail on its historic flight on December 17, 1903. Orville was lying on the wing, controlling the plane. John T. Daniels used the camera owned by Orville and Wilbur to capture the moment on film.

This time, the Wright brothers would begin their flight on level ground. They would not depend on the Flyer's sliding down a dune to pick up speed. To truly qualify as a controlled, heavier-than-air, manned flight, the motor would have to lift the plane and land at the same level of ground—not higher, not lower. The men pegged down the wooden rail along a flat place in the sand.

The Wright brothers recorded the event in many ways. A large box camera was aimed at the end of the guiding rail. Aboard the plane, instruments recorded the distance through the air, the speed, the power used, and the number of turns of the propeller. A stopwatch kept track of the time.

It was Orville Wright's turn to pilot the plane. At 10:35 A.M., the Flyer began to move along the rail. Wilbur ran alongside the right wing. Again, the plane rose into the air at the forty-foot point along the rail. John Daniels, stationed at the camera, caught the moment on film. It is probably one of the most famous pictures ever taken.

The Flyer was still hard to control. Over and over, the plane jerked up as high as ten feet and then dove back toward the ground. One hundred twenty feet from the takeoff point, a skid caught the sand and cracked, dragging the Flyer to a halt. It had flown under its own power for twelve seconds and had landed at a point as high as its takeoff point. The first controlled, heavier-than-air, manned flight had succeeded!

At 11:20 A.M., Wilbur guided the plane on a fifteen-second flight for one hundred seventy-five feet. At 11:40, Orville flew two hundred feet in the same amount of time.

Wilbur took off on the fourth flight precisely at noon on December 17, 1903. The wind was still strong but not as brisk. Again, the Flyer moved jerkily up and down. However, after three hundred feet, the flight path smoothed out for nearly eight hundred feet. Suddenly, the Flyer began bobbing again. It swooped to the ground. Wilbur had flown for 59 seconds, covering 852 feet.

The frame holding the small elevator wings in front of the plane broke during the landing. Still, the excited men talked about the possibility of flying the four miles to Kitty Hawk.

They never had a chance to try. A gust of wind flipped the Flyer. Both Orville and John Daniels made a grab for it. Daniels became tangled in the wires as the plane rolled over and over across the beach. Before it hit the ocean, Daniels broke nearly every wire and strut trying to escape. He remembered, "I ate sand for a whole week after that."[3] The Flyer was ruined.

After the group had walked back to Kitty Hawk, Orville sent a telegraph message to their family in Dayton. It was time to tell the press that powered flight had been successful. The age of aviation had finally begun.

Chapter 2

THE BISHOP'S BOYS

Wilbur and Orville Wright got their mechanical abilities from their mother. Susan Koerner Wright was the handy one in the family. Their father, Milton Wright, could not even hammer a nail in straight.

Susan Wright could fix or mend anything. She made toys for her children. She made her housework easier by using one tool for many jobs. She taught all her children to cook, sew, and use hand tools. Like her sons, Wilbur and Orville, she had the ability to see how something might work before it was built.

She inherited this mechanical aptitude from her father, John G. Koerner, a German immigrant. In the early 1800s, he improved farm wagons and carriages in Virginia and in pioneer settlements in Indiana. Susan was his fifth child, born on April 30, 1831.

On the other hand, Orville and Wilbur inherited their precise attention to recording details from their father. Milton Wright was born on November 17, 1828, in Indiana. His parents came from England. He became a preacher for the Church of the United Brethren in Christ, a small Protestant group.

Milton and Susan met at Hartsville College in Indiana. Susan Catherine Koerner, one of the few college-educated women of her time, was also a member of the United Brethren Church. They married on Thanksgiving Day, 1859.

As a preacher in the United Brethren faith, Milton Wright taught his children a belief in honesty and fair dealing. He also encouraged the development of strong character and sureness of purpose.

Milton Wright studied the history of his family. However, he discovered that relatives often made up stories about family history. Assuming that his descendants would be interested in the truth, he decided to document his own life. He kept careful track of his activities and those of his family in diaries for half a century. The importance of keeping an exact record was passed along to his children.

Family

Susan Koerner Wright was painfully shy. As her husband became more prominent within the church, she immersed herself in family life. Milton Wright was proud of her quiet modesty.[1]

Her family kept her busy. She and Milton had seven children. The two oldest boys—Reuchlin, born March 17, 1861, and Lorin, born November 18, 1862—were always close friends. Twins, Otis and Ida, were born on March 7, 1870, but died within months.

Wilbur, a middle child born on April 16, 1867, grew closer to the next two younger children—Orville, born on August 19, 1871, and Katharine, born on August 19, 1874.

In 1869, Milton Wright became the editor of the weekly United Brethren Church newspaper, The Religious Telescope. In 1877, he became a bishop of the West Mississippi District. Milton was opposed to the sale of hard liquor. He was in favor of women being allowed to vote. These progressive ideas were not widely held in the United States at that time.

The Wrights encouraged their children to do their own thinking and come to their own conclusions by searching for information in books. Their parents even told them they could take off from school whenever they wanted to pursue their own interests! The children had to earn their own money to spend on hobbies and experiments.

Both Wilbur and Orville had an early interest in mechanical toys. One of Orville's presents on his fifth birthday was a gyroscopic top. This amazing toy could stay balanced on the edge of a knife blade for as long as it could keep spinning.

Both Wright parents lovingly protected their children from the outside world that did not hold their religious beliefs. The children grew up close to their parents and to one another.

The church frequently transferred Milton Wright. Susan Wright packed and moved her family twelve times. When Milton was moved to Dayton, Ohio, they bought a house at 7 Hawthorn Street.

Orville entered kindergarten in 1876. However, when his mother visited the school a month later to see how he was getting along, the teacher was surprised to see her. Orville had not attended class since the first day. He had gone to the house of his best friend, Edwin Henry Sines, instead. From then on, Wilbur walked Orville to school.

Early Flying Attempts

In 1878, Orville's teacher, Ida Palmer, found him playing with several pieces of wood at his desk instead of doing his school assignment. He told her he was making a flying machine. If it worked, he planned to build a larger one and fly with his brother Wilbur.

The toy that inspired them to want to fly was the Pénaud helicopter their father had brought home. Orville wrote, "We built a number of copies of this toy, which flew successfully. . . . But when we undertook to build a toy on a much larger scale it failed to work so well. . . . we finally abandoned the experiments."[2]

Discovery—Curved Wings Work Better

Since the Wright children had to pay for their own supplies, Orville cut the wooden strips that formed the kites' shape into very thin strips. He could get more strips out of a block of wood this way. These strips bent when the kite flew, creating a curved surface. The curved kites flew much better than traditional kites made with sturdier wooden bars.

Orville also built kites. He started a successful business selling his kites to other children in order to earn spending money.

Injury and Disease

The five Wright children survived the usual childhood diseases. Unfortunately, Susan Wright developed tuberculosis in 1883. At that time, there was no cure for this disease of the lungs.

In January 1886, Wilbur was hurt playing shinny (a game like ice hockey). A shinny stick slipped out of one boy's hand and slammed into Wilbur's face. It knocked nineteen-year-old Wilbur down and punched out his front teeth. It took Wilbur a long time to recover from this accident. He also developed a heart disorder and stomach problems and became depressed.

While he recovered, Susan Wright gradually became a helpless invalid. Milton Wright could not resign from his church duties to care for her. Reuchlin was married and had a family of his own. Lorin was not available to help, either. He had traveled to Kansas to seek his fortune. Fifteen-year-old Orville and twelve-year-old Katharine were still in school.

Wilbur had finished high school but had not gone to college. He was the logical person to care for their mother. Caring for his mother brought Wilbur out of his depression and also gave him time to do lots of reading. He studied ancient and modern history, current events, literature, ethics, and science. He had an inquisitive mind and an extraordinary memory.

Conflict in the Church

In May 1889, Bishop Milton Wright's church conference adopted a new constitution. Milton and his followers fought against the change but were defeated. Instead of accepting this decision, they broke away from the church to form a new one—the Church of the United Brethren in Christ (Old Constitution). Naturally, Milton Wright became the head of this new group.

The old congregation and the new breakaway group spent the next few years in court, suing and countersuing each other over the ownership of church property and various religious ideals. Wilbur helped his father write editorials and pamphlets defending his views. The whole family became firm believers in the role of law and the courts to prove the rightness of a cause.

The Family Bonds Tighten

On July 4, 1889, Susan Koerner Wright died—three years after Wilbur had begun taking care of her. Devastated, Milton Wright wrote in his diary that the light had gone out of his home.[3]

With his wife dead, his two older children long since moved away, and his church in conflict, Milton grew more demanding of his three remaining children. He worked to protect them by teaching them that the world outside was filled with people who were not to be trusted.

In Business Together

That September, Orville did not attend his last year of high school. He decided to take just one Latin course at school, instead. He felt this would better prepare him for college. During the rest of the day, he concentrated on his printing business.

He and Ed Sines had traded a collection of magazines for a printing press. The two boys earned money by printing handbills,

Paul Laurence Dunbar

Paul Laurence Dunbar became a famous poet and novelist by the early 1900s. He was the first African American to become nationally known as a poet and writer of fiction. Three of his poetry collections are Lyrics of Lowly Life *(1896),* Lyrics of the Hearthside *(1899), and* Lyrics of Love and Laughter *(1903). He was only thirty-four years old when he died on February 9, 1906.*

advertising posters, business cards, and tickets. They turned out such quality work that Wilbur took notice. Wilbur had his brother publish church pamphlets plus his other writings.

In 1889, Wilbur joined Orville in running the print shop. They called it "Wright Bros.: Job Printers at 7 Hawthorn Street."

Soon the Wright brothers built an even larger printing press. In March 1889, the Wrights began publishing a weekly newspaper called the West Side News.

Ed Sines sold advertising and operated the press. Wilbur became the editor; Orville the publisher. The two brothers created a solid working partnership. Humor was a big part of their relationship. Being brothers, Wilbur and Orville argued all the time. However, they had learned to sprinkle their arguments with humor. This kept arguments from becoming explosive and hateful.

One of the contributors to the West Side News was a former high school classmate of Orville's, Paul Laurence Dunbar, who would later become a famous African-American poet. One day, Dunbar scribbled a poem on the wall of the Wrights' shop:

Orville Wright is out of sight
In the printing business.
No other mind is half so bright
As his'n is.[4]

The Wright boys also published The Tattler, a newspaper Dunbar produced for the African-American community. They printed it on credit. Because it earned no profit, they could afford to produce only three issues.

The printing firm, now called Wright & Wright, continued to be successful, but Wilbur and Orville Wright were bored. They looked around for another business to get involved in and found . . . bicycles.

Chapter 3

IN BUSINESS WITH BICYCLES

When bicycles were first invented in France in the 1790s, they were called wooden horses. They were difficult to ride. The rider sat between two wooden wheels, which could not be steered, and pushed the bicycle along with his feet. Later, a movable front wheel gave the rider steering control. Pedals attached by a chain to the back wheel made it easier to move fast.

In the 1860s, the French invented the velocipede. It had a large front wheel and a tiny back wheel. The larger the wheel, the faster it could go. By the 1870s, the front wheel, above which the rider sat, was often five feet high. However, the rough dirt roads with stones and potholes caused many accidents.

The Wright brothers became interested in one of the world's greatest inventions—the "safety bicycle." This bicycle, invented in 1885, had two wheels of equal size with rubber tires. With the addition of two- and three-speed hub gears, it could now be used by anyone. It was almost as fast as a horse, and faster than a horse-drawn wagon. This was as close to flying as a person could get.

Wilbur Wright at work in the bicycle repair shop. In 1893, the Wright brothers opened a bicycle shop with a showroom and repair shop.

Both of the Wright brothers enjoyed bicycling. Wilbur preferred long country rides. Orville dove into track racing, winning three races. Both developed skills as bicycle mechanics.

Bicycle Business

In 1893, Wilbur and Orville opened a bicycle shop called the Wright Cycle Exchange, with a showroom and a repair shop. Soon they carried the best bicycles on the market for rent and for sale. Ed Sines helped them.

A few automobiles appeared in Dayton, but the brothers did not see how anyone could make a living working with them. The rich people who owned them also hired their own mechanics to work on them. They predicted they would make a better living working on bicycles.

Business boomed. In the fall of 1893, they moved to a larger place and renamed it the Wright Cycle Company. For the rest of their lives, Wilbur and Orville maintained a joint bank account. All the money they earned went into it. Each brother took out whatever amount he needed.

Wilbur later wrote that

From the time we were little children, my brother Orville and myself lived together, played together, worked together, and, in fact, thought together.... [We] talked over our thoughts and aspirations so that nearly everything that was done in our lives has been the result of conversations, suggestions, and discussions between us.[1]

In 1895, the two brothers decided to manufacture their own bicycles. They designed a new type of wheel hub and coaster brake. First they needed to create machinery to run the tools that manufactured the bicycle parts. The brothers built an engine powered by gasoline, instead of the more dangerous steam, to run their lathe. Each Wright bicycle was hand built, piece by piece—using the tools attached to their lathe—for every customer.

Bicycles kept the brothers busy during the spring and summer, but fall was slow and winter dull. They spent the winter reconditioning old bicycles or manufacturing new ones. In their spare time, they read.

Interest in Flight

Wilbur wrote: "My own active interest in aeronautical problems dates back to the death of Lilienthal in 1896. . . . [His death notice] aroused an . . . interest which had existed from my childhood. . . ."[2]

Many people had flown gliders. A glider is a heavier-than-air aircraft with no engine. Early gliders could not stay up in the air very long. Many people thought that if they could only use a glider to hover like birds, perhaps they could someday learn to move in the air.

Most nineteenth-century gliders crashed. But one German glider enthusiast, Otto Lilienthal, seemed to be solving some of the problems of flight. Lilienthal became the first person in aviation history to manufacture gliders for sale.

On August 9, 1896, Lilienthal was testing a new glider when it stalled in the air. He fell fifty feet to his death.

Orville knew nothing about Lilienthal's death. He had fallen sick with typhoid from drinking polluted water. Orville almost died. To keep Orville's spirits up while he slowly recovered, Wilbur talked to him about Lilienthal's experiments.

The brothers looked for other books about flight but found very little. Most newspaper articles laughed at the "crackpots" who attempted and failed to fly. Some had tried wings that flapped like birds'. Others created paddle wheels for the air like those on the riverboats that steamed down the rivers. Still others shaped their wings like fish or even spirals. None worked.

In a few months, when Orville had fully recovered, the brothers returned to the bicycle business. During the winters, they talked (and argued) about the problems of flight. They watched birds in the air and wondered. It was not until 1899 that the Wright brothers discovered the marvelous advances that happened during the 1890s.

During the winter of 1899, they came upon a translation of a French work on bird flight in the Dayton Public Library called L'Empire de l'Air by Louis-Pierre Mouillard. Wilbur called this work "one of the inspiring causes in the efforts of the Wright brothers."[3] Orville later wrote, "If the bird's wings would sustain

Lilienthal's Technique

Otto Lilienthal controlled his glider by dangling his body between the wings and shifting his weight. This action shifted the center of gravity and moved the glider slowly in the direction he wanted to go. It was clumsy and not very accurate.

it in the air without the use of any muscular effort, we did not see why man could not be sustained by the same means."[4]

The translation had been in an annual report of the Smithsonian Institution. On May 30, 1899, Wilbur wrote to the Smithsonian in Washington, D.C., asking for advice about studying the art of flight. He assured them that he was a serious researcher: ". . . I am an enthusiast, but not a crank. . . . I wish to avail myself of all that is already known and then if possible add my mite [my little bit] to help on the future worker who will attain final success. . . ."[5]

Early Flight Experimenters

Wilbur's request was only one of many. The Smithsonian sent a few pamphlets plus a list of suggested books. In this way, Wilbur and Orville learned that Samuel Pierpont Langley, the secretary of the Smithsonian, had experimented with flight in May 1896. Langley had attached twin propellers powered by a small, lightweight steam engine to model flying machines he called aerodromes.

Langley launched seven of these experimental craft from a houseboat on the Potomac River near Quantico, Virginia. Most sank. However, the fifth circled the houseboat twice, going higher and higher up to one hundred feet in the air. After ninety seconds, it ran out of steam. It drifted down to float on the river. This was the first successful machine-driven flight of a heavier-than-air craft.

Langley built a larger version of the model—one he hoped would be large enough to carry a man aloft. In 1898, he received a grant of fifty thousand dollars from the United States Army Board of Ordnance and Fortification to cover the costs.

The Wright brothers also discovered another scientist, Octave Chanute, a retired engineer. His book, describing the history of modern attempts to fly up to 1894, was called Progress in Flying Machines.

Chanute had experimented with gliders on the sand dunes of the Lake Michigan shore in Indiana. One had six pairs of wings. His most successful glider was a biplane (with two wings). These wings were connected by solid struts (pieces of wood) with wires crisscrossing between the wings and the struts, creating a flexible, but solid, unit.

Wilbur, with Orville's support, wrote to Chanute and Langley about their experiments. Chanute responded. He always encouraged people who were interested in his hobby. Over the next ten years, he became one of the Wright brothers' greatest supporters.

The Wright Brothers Enter the Field

Once the brothers began tinkering with flight, they stopped manufacturing their own bicycles, but continued to sell and repair other brands. The profits from the bicycle business would pay for their research about flight.

They used modern engineering methods in their quest. They identified the problem—manned flight—and then defined it. In their studies, they discovered missing bits of information. They then knew which problems had already been solved. All they needed to do was list the problems yet to be solved. The main problem was control.

Control While Flying

While moving forward, an automobile needs only to control turning either left or right. On a glider or plane, this is called yaw.

A bicycle, on the other hand, can roll over onto its side if the rider loses balance. Therefore, on a bicycle, the rider must control not only left and right, but also a sideways roll. On a plane this is also called roll.

Flying in the air adds another dimension to this. The airplane needs to control pitch as well. Pitch is the movement of the nose and tail up and down. Too much pitch and the plane noses down into the ground or flops over onto its back.

The Wrights discovered which experimental wings had successfully lifted into the air. A motor light enough and strong enough had already been invented. The gasoline motor could move the plane forward fast enough so that the air flowing over the wings would create enough lift. The only problem left to solve was a means of controlling the machine once it was in the air.

The smaller Langley aerodromes could make wide, flat turns in the air by using a rear rudder. A pilot would have very little control of balance. The aerodrome's wingtips automatically stabilized the machine.

Wilbur and Orville searched for a way to allow the pilot to balance and control every maneuver of the aircraft. A rider stays balanced on a bicycle by leaning into a turn. How could the pilot control the balance of the wings?

Tom D. Crouch, curator of astronautics at the National Air and Space Museum, said that Wilbur's genius was the ability to study the principles of bicycling and conclude that they would also apply to aeronautics. Since "what [Wilbur] could see and feel, he would understand," he looked for a mechanical control to the problem.[6]

The brothers had seen birds circle in the air by changing the positions of their wing feathers—the tip of one wing curved down while the tip of the other curved up. How could men do this with fabric-covered wood?

One July day, Wilbur had just sold an inner tube to a customer. He picked up the lightweight rectangular box that had contained the bicycle inner tube. It was about a foot long, an inch or so high, and a couple of inches wide. While he talked to the customer, he began absentmindedly twisting the box with both hands.

All at once he noticed what he was doing. His mind suddenly connected what he had noticed birds doing in flight—changing the shape and position of the tips of their wings—with the action of the twisting box.

Wilbur had found a mechanical way to control roll. He hurried to show Orville. He tore off the ends of the box to make the flexing action more clear. The brothers excitedly concluded that if they took the wings of a Chanute double-deck glider and rearranged the wires, the pilot could twist the wings and control roll.

In an article called "How We Invented the Airplane," Orville later wrote, "in flying, the wings on the right and left sides could be warped so as to present their surfaces to the air at different angles of incidence and thus secure unequal lifts on the two sides. . . ."[7] The Wright brothers' unique idea was that the twist would be applied across the whole wing structure. When one end curved down, the other end would curve up. This control was the basis of the Wright patent. This idea had never been considered by earlier flight experimenters.[8]

In August 1899, some of the neighborhood boys helped Wilbur test his new small two-winged glider- kite in a nearby open area. The double wings of this kite were five feet from tip to tip. Wires held in his other hand controlled the twisting or warping of the wings. It worked.

Now all they had to do was build a larger glider- kite—one that could carry a man.

Chapter 4

EXPERIMENTS
WITH GLIDERS

ewspapers and magazines at this time carried articles by professors and scientists that seemed to prove it would be impossible to build a flying machine that would carry a man. The brothers ignored these articles. They quietly prepared for their first flight attempts.

Wilbur Wright was thirty-three years old. His family called him Will. His younger brother, Orville (often called Orv), was twenty-nine. Orville was shy. Wilbur, who loved to talk, was their contact with the outside world.

Neither brother was comfortable around women his own age. As a result, the brothers were perfectly content to live at home with their sister, Katharine, taking care of them and the house. She took over the responsibility for the household when their mother died in 1889. She had graduated from Oberlin College in 1898 and was now teaching at Steele High School in Dayton. To help with the household chores, Katharine hired a part-time servant, Carrie Kayler, who remained with the family for decades.

Bishop Milton Wright spent many weeks of the year away from home, visiting churches. Reuchlin would return home to visit occasionally. Their brother Lorin and his four children lived down the street.

Children

Wilbur and Orville Wright loved children but felt no need for their own. They simply invited their nieces and nephews to visit. Some evenings Uncle Will and Uncle Orv organized magic lantern shows, which used an early form of slides lit by an oil lantern. Other times they made candy with their young nieces and nephews. They made puppets from sheet metal with moving legs and arms for shadow puppet shows. They made helicopters for the children out of bamboo, paper, corks, and rubber bands.

Niece Ivonette remembered being dropped off at her uncles' bicycle shop while her mother ran errands. She remembered that the shop was always a fascinating, noisy place with "motors being tested on the block, and wheels and belts running."[1]

Nephew Milton was attracted by "The odor of the glue pot, the spruce shavings on the floor, and the many gadgets whose use I did not understand."[2] He thought all bicycle shops made "flying machines" just like his uncles' shop did.

Both Ivonette and Milton remembered their uncles' discussions. The two men were so close that they could toss ideas back and forth in partial sentences—sometimes calmly, often shouting. They enjoyed arguing. Wilbur once said, "I love to scrap with Orv, he's such a good scrapper."[3] At times they would swap sides and begin arguing the other's side of the issue.

Search for a Place

In the fall of 1899, Wilbur and Orville decided they needed a place with stronger winds than Dayton to fly the new, larger glider they planned to build. The place had to have many rain-free days, plus a large open area. Wilbur wrote to the United

States Weather Bureau in Washington, D.C., for advice. Was there a place in the United States with winds that blew constantly strong and steady?

Among the places the Weather Bureau suggested was the Outer Banks—a series of long, narrow peninsulas and barrier islands along the Atlantic Coast just off North Carolina. The weather station at a small town called Kitty Hawk reported winds averaging about sixteen miles per hour. The brothers decided this was the closest place to Dayton, Ohio, that would have enough constant wind to help lift the glider.

Encouragement

In the spring of 1900, Wilbur first contacted Octave Chanute about his interest in flight. By May, Wilbur had received a letter of encouragement from Chanute. He also sent a copy of Otto Lilienthal's air-pressure tables, which flight experimenters of the day used to determine how large a glider's wings should be and what amount of curve they should have to be able to lift off. That summer the Wrights, guided by Lilienthal's tables, constructed a glider large enough to carry a person.

Kitty Hawk

Wilbur wrote to the Kitty Hawk postmaster, Bill Tate, asking about possible locations for their flight experiments. Tate suggested a place called Kill Devil Hills, four miles south of the town of Kitty Hawk. It had three tall sand dunes they could use as jump-off points.

Wilbur left for the Outer Banks on September 6, 1900. Orville followed later. Wilbur wrote his father,

> . . . It is my belief that flight is possible and while I am taking up the investigation for pleasure rather than profit, I think there is a slight chance of achieving fame and fortune from it. . . . I am certain I can reach a point much in advance of any previous workers in this field even if complete success is not attained at present. . . .[4]

The brothers had planned to use eighteen-foot pine spars (lengths of wood) for the glider's wings. However, only sixteen-foot spars were available in North Carolina. Therefore, Wilbur needed to cut a section out of the middle of the sateen fabric wing covering. Wilbur refused to ask others to work on his aeronautic project. He preferred to do it himself and know it was done right. He carried the Tates' sewing machine into the yard to sew the fabric together himself.

With the extra curved pieces on the ends, the final wingspan of the 1900 glider was seventeen feet, five inches. The pilot would lie on the bottom wing, causing less wind resistance.

Orville arrived on September 28. By the end of the month, the brothers began their flight tests on the beach near Kitty Hawk. Wilbur could not wait. He lay down on the bottom glider wing and attempted a short flight that first day. Orville and Bill Tate handled the lines. For a short time, the glider remained a few feet off the ground. Then it swooped up to a height of fifteen feet and began to dart and bob around. Wilbur's reaction to the experience of flying was to shout, "Let me down!"[5] He had been in the air only a few minutes.

The two brothers then moved half a mile south of Kitty Hawk. They lived in a tent. A fall storm buried the glider under several wagon loads of sand. It took a day to dig it out.

The brothers discovered that they had misunderstood the United States Weather Bureau's wind information. The wind here did not blow constantly at sixteen miles per hour every day. The Weather Bureau had given them the average wind speed for the month, not the daily speed. Some days the wind blew sixty miles per hour and on other days only ten. They discovered that, because their glider's wings were shorter than they had planned, they needed a steady wind of twenty-five miles an hour to lift the glider into the air.

They flew the full-sized glider just as they had flown their smaller gliders. One man, usually Wilbur, stood on the sand, holding lines attached to the glider, guiding it. Orville and Bill

Tate lifted it and threw it into the wind. Tate began packing a full day's work into a few hours so he could spend the rest of the day helping the Wrights. His half brother, Dan, also helped when he could.

Wilbur did not fly again until close to the end of their stay. For the next few weeks, the brothers flew the glider like a kite. They tried placing the wings at different angles. They tried a flexible tail. Then they moved the horizontal tail pieces to the front of the glider and called them elevators. The brothers thought this front elevator was their most important invention.[6]

The smaller single-winged elevator in front tipped up and down, controlling the pitch of the glider. It made the glider more stable. Plus it prevented the danger of a nosedive into the ground. At this point, the glider had no rear rudder.

The brothers tied lengths of chain on the glider to test how much weight it could carry. Among their equipment was the very best camera on the market—a Korona-V. It cost eighty-five dollars—six times the expense of the wood and fabric of the glider. With this camera, the invention of the airplane would be fully documented on film.

Brothers on Vacation

Even though the Wright brothers kept good written records of almost every experiment in later years, in 1900 they did not. This first year they acted like boys on vacation. They used the camera mostly for fun. They took pictures of the people and places on the Outer Banks, but only three of the 1900 glider. They made few written records as well. However, over the next few years, their records and photographs became more detailed.

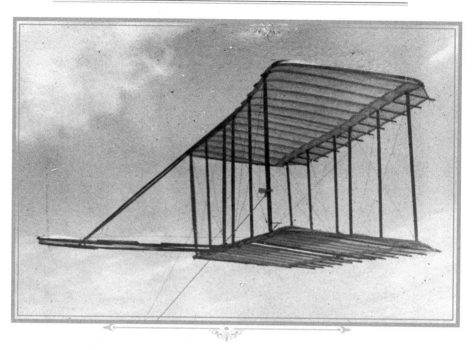

In their early tests, the Wrights flew this 1900 glider as a kite. Wind warping was controlled from the ground by a set of strings.

Manned Glider

By October, they were ready to see whether the glider could carry a person. However, for several days, the winds were only ten miles per hour—too light to lift a grown man's weight. Dan Tate's seventy-pound son, Tom, volunteered to fly.

Ten-year-old Tom eagerly climbed aboard. His father and Orville lifted the glider into the air. The wind caught it. Wilbur controlled the lines, causing the glider to swoop, climb, and glide. It reached ten feet above the sand.

On October 18, the men practiced free glides. They threw the glider off a sand dune with no lines attached and let it float to the ground. Several times it suddenly turned and crashed into the sand dune. The Wrights strapped the broken struts together, then threw it off the dune again.

It was time to return to Dayton. Katharine had fired the man the brothers had left in charge of the bicycle shop. They had a business to run and their vacation was almost over.

On their last day at the Outer Banks in October, the Wrights took the glider south to the three tall Kill Devil Hills dunes. There is no record about the height of the dunes that year, but they were probably between fifty and one hundred feet tall. (Sand dunes change in size, depending on winds and storms.)

Wilbur climbed aboard and lay down on the lower wing of the glider. Bill Tate and Orville ran the glider down the big dune, holding the tips of the wings until it lifted out of their reach. The elevator control worked perfectly. Wilbur flew five feet above the sand, landing three to four hundred feet away.

He had controlled the whole flight with the elevator—not by swinging his legs as other glider pilots did. The only danger Wilbur encountered was the mouthful of sand he got when the lower wing he was lying on slid along the sand as the glider came to a stop. He made several more flights that day.

The brothers left the glider on the sand dune and returned to Dayton. They told the Tates they could have the glider. From their observations, the brothers knew that they would need to build a glider with a different shape next year.

Chapter 5

TRUSTING THEIR OWN CALCULATIONS

In 1901, Wilbur and Orville spent July and part of August on the Outer Banks. They changed the curve of the wings of their glider. This summer's glider was the largest anyone had ever tried to fly. They stored it in a specially built wooden shed near Kill Devil Hills. The brothers set up camp in part of the shed. Orville wrote to Katharine, complaining about the mosquitoes and sand fleas.

Wilbur continued to correspond with Octave Chanute. Chanute worried about the Wright brothers living all alone, so far from civilization. He sent George A. Spratt to help them. Spratt had some medical training and was interested in aeronautics. Chanute also dropped in for a few days to observe the experiments.

The brothers discovered their new, larger machine did not fly as well as last year's model. When they reduced the arc of the wings, it flew better, but it was still hard to control. It would stop its forward movement, lose the lift under its wings, and drop out of the sky. This is called a stall. Wilbur, the pilot, would end up with a mouthful of sand, a bruised nose, or a black eye. (Wilbur, protective of his little brother, refused to allow Orville to fly until they had figured out how to do it safely. Too many people had died trying to control gliders in the past years.)

Their North Carolina experiments of 1900 and 1901 proved that the Lilienthal tables of air pressure on curved surfaces were not accurate. The Wright brothers' glider's wings did not produce anywhere near the lift that Otto Lilienthal's tables had said they should. The Wrights realized they would have to compile tables of their own.

In mid-August 1901, they returned to Dayton by train, extremely discouraged. Wilbur was ready to stop trying. He told Orville, "Not within a thousand years would man ever fly!"[1]

Chanute, however, continued to encourage the brothers. As far as he could tell, no one else was as close to flying as they were. His enthusiasm inspired them to try again.

The First Announcement of Their Flights

Chanute invited the brothers to give a talk to a group called the Western Society of Engineers. Shy Orville refused. Katharine nagged Wilbur into giving the speech. On September 18, 1901, Wilbur addressed the group.

Normally, Wilbur did not care what he wore. Orville was the fashionable one. Katharine wrote to her father: "We had a picnic getting Will off to Chicago. Orv offered all his clothes, so off went [Wilbur] arrayed in Orv's shirt, collars, cuffs, cuff links and overcoat. We discovered that to some extent 'clothes do make the man' for you never saw Will look so 'swell!'"[2]

In his speech, Wilbur announced for the first time in public that the current tables of air pressure seemed to contain errors.

Testing Wing Designs

When Wilbur returned to Dayton, he and Orville began a series of tests that would enable them to create a more accurate table of air pressure. First, they cut pieces of thin metal into various small wing shapes. The brothers then set the metal shapes, which they called vanes, in the yard where wind could blow over them. They watched to see which shape created more lift. However, just using Dayton breezes was unsatisfactory. They needed stronger winds.

To create a stronger breeze, the brothers tried fixing the vanes on a bicycle wheel rim attached to the handle of a bicycle. By traveling at a fast, steady speed down the street, they could see and measure the air pressure on these vanes.

The Lilienthal table predicted the lift should have been at an angle of 5 degrees. The brothers' tests, however, showed it was closer to 18 degrees. This proved that the Lilienthal tables of air pressure were wrong. Everyone had been using the wrong information. No wonder no one had been able to fly yet.

For an even more controlled test, they set up a small wind tunnel in their bicycle shop, pushing air through it with a fan. They placed the fan on a separate stand. This way, the vibration of the fan would not shake the experimental vanes. The fan pushed air through an open-ended rectangular box about six feet long with an opening sixteen inches square. The air blew through a piece of sheet metal pierced with holes—to straighten the flow—into the wind tunnel. The Wrights could watch what happened to the wing shapes by looking through a pane of glass on the top of the box.

Over the next few months, the Wright brothers tested more than two hundred types of wing surfaces, curves, and angles. They created more than fifty model wings made of tin, galvanized iron, twenty-gage steel, solder, and wax. The brothers took careful notes about their observations. When they were done, they had a complete, accurate table of air pressure.

Their results proved the opposite of what was currently believed to be true. Professor Samuel Langley had built his Great Aerodrome around the belief that a sharp leading edge would cut the air with less wind resistance. The Wrights discovered that a blunt rounded edge—with the sharper edge to the rear of the wing—worked better and created more lift.

While they were putting their flying machine together in the fall of 1903, Orville and Wilbur practiced with the 1902 glider. This photograph was taken from the top of one of the Kill Devil Hills sand dunes.

Chanute sent copies of the results of the brothers' tests to his friends. Chanute was always generous about sharing information. The Wrights, however, had not given him permission to do so. They wanted to test these air pressure tables with gliders of their own before announcing their results.

Orville was thrilled with their new discoveries about air pressure. He said, "It suggested that maybe the reason others had failed to fly was not because the thing couldn't be done."[3] It may have been because people were working with the wrong data.

During the busy bicycle business season in the spring of 1902, the brothers designed a new wing shape for their glider. They also added a stationary rudder with twin vertical vanes in the back of the plane. This would control the sideways slide that happened when the wings were warped.

On August 20, 1902, Katharine wrote her father: "Will spins the sewing machine around by the hour while Orv squats around marking the places to sew [the wing covering]."[4] Although she complained about the noise, she knew she would be lonely when her brothers left the next week.

Back to the Outer Banks, 1902

Both men loved going to the Outer Banks. They kept assuring Katharine that life at Kitty Hawk cured all ills. They sent souvenirs home to Lorin's children. Lorin's son, Milton, remembered receiving a dried horseshoe crab from his uncles, along with bottles of seawater and sand.

This year, Wilbur taught Orville to fly, shouting instructions from the ground. By September 21, 1902, Orville had flown fifty times. On September 23, the glider stalled and crashed to the ground. Orville crawled out of the mess without a single scratch.

Several of the crashes had been tailspins. After another crash on October 3, the brothers changed the twin tail vanes to a single one.

They also redesigned the arrangement of the wires holding the two wings together. Now the wires would hold the center part of the wings firmly, allowing only the ends of the wings to warp up and down as they piloted the plane. The center of the flying machine would have to be strong and stable if it were to hold a heavy engine plus a pilot.

By the time the Wright brothers left the Outer Banks on October 28, 1902, they had solved most of the problems of flight. The pilot now had the three-dimensional control necessary for flight in the air—control of roll, pitch, and yaw.

This year they had broken all records for a glider. They had flown the largest glider. By gliding over 550 feet, they had made the longest distance glide. Wilbur had spent the longest time gliding in the air—twenty-six seconds, on October 23. They had flown in the strongest winds and had used the smallest angle of descent.[5]

A New Propeller Design

That winter, they created propellers to push the aircraft along. They also created an efficient motor to run the propellers on their heavier-than-air craft, which they planned to call the Flyer.

At this time, propellers used flat blades welded at a sharp angle to the cylinder that attached it to the boat or air machine. People thought they acted in the water (or air) like a screw drilling into wood. By experimenting with different shapes and angles, they discovered that a propeller is not like a screw. It is a rotating wing. Therefore, instead of flat blades with sharp edges on both sides, the Wrights created a propeller with a rounded edge on the forward side of the blade. Then they sanded a smooth concave arch along the blade and mounted them at an angle. These propeller blades are still in use today.

A Lightweight Motor

The brothers, with the assistance of Charlie Taylor, who helped out in their bicycle shop, built their own motor for the Flyer. This lightweight engine produced over twelve horsepower.

The engine was bolted in the middle of the Flyer. Its motion was transferred to the propellers by bicycle chains. The two propellers turned in opposite directions. They were attached behind the wing and pushed the plane along.

Patent Application

Wilbur filed their first patent application on March 23, 1903. This application did not talk about the motor. It simply set down the basic principles used to control and guide their Flyer—the wing warping system.

The United States Patent Office was tired of crackpot applications for flying machines. In the 1890s, they decided to reject all flying machine applications unless the person could demonstrate that the machine had actually flown. They rejected the Wrights' patent application for these reasons:

1. *The drawings were inadequate.*

2. *The written description was vague and indefinite.*

3. *At least six other recent patents claimed the same thing.*

4. *The thing described was clearly inoperative and "incapable of performing its intended function."*[6]

The Wright brothers knew their Flyer would work. They had already flown the basic design as a glider. All they needed was a good, lightweight engine plus an efficient propeller to make it self-propelled instead of wind-dependent. They had already solved the problems of flight control. It was the flight control method they were trying to patent.

Wilbur sent the patent office a cardboard inner tube box to illustrate their wing warping technique of flight control. But without Wilbur standing in front of them to demonstrate, the men at the patent office did not understand how it would work. The application was rejected again.

Back to the Outer Banks, 1903

Each of the previous years, the Wright brothers had left behind their experimental gliders on the Outer Banks. They did not need their old machines because each year they built a new machine, incorporating all the improvements they felt they needed.

In 1903, the brothers built their new machine inside their shed near Kill Devil Hills. This time, they stretched the cloth over both the top and bottom sides of the spars and ribs of the wings. It created a smooth surface on both the upper and lower sides of each wing. This smooth wing surface reduced wind resistance and drag. It was the first double-surfaced plane ever built.

The pilot wedged his hips into a small wooden box called a hip cradle. When he wiggled his hips, the movement activated lines controlling the wing warping and rudder. A hand control moved the elevator (the small wings in front of the main part of the plane) up and down. There was no way to make the engine go faster, but the pilot did have a cutoff switch. This would immediately make the Flyer a glider—and they already knew they could fly gliders.

Weighing more than seven hundred pounds, the Flyer was too heavy to simply throw off a sand dune. Besides, they wanted to prove that the machine could lift itself. Therefore, it had to lift off and land on a flat surface.

The Wright brothers were not fully set up until mid-October. It was on December 17 that the Wright brothers succeeded, making the world's first manned, power-driven, heavier-than-air flight. This year, the brothers would not abandon their experimental aircraft on the sands of the Outer Banks. They carefully packed the Flyer in boxes and shipped it home to Dayton.

Their telegram to their father, Bishop Milton Wright, said: "Success four flights thursday morning all against twenty one mile wind started from Level with engine power alone average speed through air thirty one miles longest 57 seconds inform Press home #### Christmas."[7] (The actual time recorded was 59 seconds.)

In Dayton, their older brother, Lorin Wright, took the telegram to the Dayton Herald newspaper. Reporter Frank Tunison told Lorin, "Fifty-seven seconds, hey? If it had been fifty-seven minutes then it might have been a news item."[8] This statement is now a legend in newspaper circles.

In those days, telegrams passed through many hands before they reached their destination. Newspapermen paid telegraph operators to pass along interesting information. A newspaper in Norfolk, Virginia, just north of the Outer Banks, picked up the few facts from that telegram and published a story about a three-mile flight. They even got the description of the Flyer wrong. The Dayton Herald and other newspapers around the nation picked up that untrue story and added their own false information.

The truth seemed like small potatoes compared with the rumors. Yet the December 17 flight was, in fact, the first step off the planet for a human being.

Chapter 6

PERFECTING THE FLYER

Wilbur and Orville Wright had already proven that a person could fly. Now they worked to make flying practical. Most of the world had no idea what the brothers were doing.

In January 1904, Wilbur sent out more press releases to correct the errors in the original stories. He also gave Octave Chanute permission to spread the word. However, Chanute told people the Wright brothers were his students and were continuing the work that he, Chanute, had begun.

Chanute's aeronautics friend, Augustus Herring, also heard the news of the successful flight. He began claiming that the brothers had used his ideas. After all, he had been with them at Kill Devil Hills in 1902 for a week. Herring wrote to Wilbur and Orville, trying to force them to recognize him as their partner. The Wrights ignored him. However, they realized that they needed to get their own patent if they wanted to prevent other claims. They hired patent lawyer Harry A. Toulmin to do the job.

What Is a Patent?

Patents are awarded by governments to individuals who have invented something new. A patent guarantees that the inventor may, for a certain period (twenty years in the United States), have the exclusive right to make, use, and sell his or her invention. At the time the Wrights patented their Flyer, patents were awarded for a period of about ten years. During the period covered by the patent, any person who wished to use this invention would have to pay the patent holder to do so.

The Wright brothers tried to get a broad patent, covering every aspect of workable flight. If they succeeded, everyone who wanted to build a flying machine would have to pay the Wrights for the right to do it.

Once they had a workable Flyer, they intended to sell it to a government. The brothers hoped flying machines might actually prevent wars.[1] They could be used to see the enemy armies' movements.

Perfecting an Airplane Near Dayton

The Wright brothers were torn in two directions. On the one hand, they wanted people to know they could fly, and they wanted to correct the tall tales that were being published. However, they could not let too many experts observe the flights and learn their secrets before they were protected by a patent.

Wilbur and Orville found a field near Dayton to do their experiments. They offered to rent it from bank president Torrence Huffman, but he allowed them to use it, for free—as long as they moved the cows living there to a safe place and did not run over them.

More than forty people came for the first flight of the Flyer II on May 23, 1904. However, the wind, which had been gusting strongly earlier, became dead calm. The brothers needed at least an eleven-mile-per-hour wind to help the plane lift off. In addition, the gasoline engine would not work properly. It just sputtered and coughed. There was no flight.

Everyone was invited to return the next day. Only a few reporters returned to see the Flyer II fly six feet off the ground for sixty feet. The brothers gave the reporters an open invitation to drop in anytime.

During that summer, there were many crashes. Every piece of the plane that could break, did. Both brothers sustained countless bumps and bruises. Neighbors sent bottles of liniment for the poor downed pilots.

The Wright brothers expected eventually to create a flying machine that could carry more than one person. However, they promised their father that they would not fly together. That way, a fatal air crash could not snuff out both their lives at once.

Ignored by Reporters

Most reporters told the Wrights they would return if anything special happened. But over the next few years, every time they asked the brothers if anything had happened, the brothers' response would be very casual—they had flown in a circle, or they had flown for six minutes. The brothers managed to keep news hounds and curious spectators from invading their privacy by acting as if nothing secret were happening. Newspapermen knew so little about aeronautics that six minutes of flight did not seem to be a big enough story to print. Even when people who saw the Wright brothers flying over Huffman Field came to the Dayton Daily News office, wondering why the paper was not covering the flights, the newspaper refused to print the stories. The owner of the newspaper, James M. Cox, said he simply did not believe anyone could fly and that was that.

On September 7, they used a derrick for the first time. This sped up and made their takeoffs safer.

One day in September 1904, several reporters came out to the field. They watched Wilbur fly down to the end of the field, turn, come back, and land safely. They saw no news there and left. They never knew they had witnessed the very first successful pilot-controlled turn in the air.

First Controlled Circle in the Air

A beekeeper named Amos Root came often to watch the men fly. On September 20, 1904, Root saw the very first complete circle made by a plane in the air. The 4,080-foot flight was completed in just over a minute and a half, but it made Root so excited he jotted down some notes:

> It was one of the grandest sights . . . of my life. Imagine a locomotive that has left its track, and is climbing up in the air right toward you—a locomotive without any wheels . . . but with white wings instead. . . . Well, now, imagine this white locomotive, with wings that spread 20 feet each way, coming right toward you with a tremendous flap of its propellers, and you will have something like what I saw.[2]

He wrote an article about it and offered it to Scientific American magazine, which refused to print it. In desperation, Root printed the article in his own magazine, Gleanings in Bee Culture, in January 1905. For the next two years, the only place a person could read about the flight experiments going on near Dayton, Ohio, was in a beekeeping magazine.

The Wright brothers added the world's first flight instrument to their Flyer II in the fall. Because the pilot could not tell how steeply the plane banked in turns, they tied a string to a crossbar. When the plane was flying level, the string blew back toward the pilot's face. But when it turned, or went up or down, the pilot could see the string pointing toward the earth. The angle of the string told them the angle of the turn.

During the next several years, most European flyers found themselves unable to repeat the Wright brothers' experiments. Drawings of the Flyer showed all the truss wires that held the plane together. But the drawings did not show the control cables that made the wings warp.

Selling the Flyer

Twice, the Wrights offered to sell their Flyer to the United States government. In 1905, they wrote that their Flyer III "flies through the air at high speed [thirty miles per hour] . . . lands without being wrecked."[3] They did not enclose any drawings or photographs.

The United States Board of Ordnance and Fortification was tired of receiving letters about unproven flying machines. The government had given Samuel Langley a lot of money for his failed flying machine. The board was determined not to throw away its money again. Both times the board replied to the Wright brothers' offer with a refusal to invest in a machine until "it has been brought to the stage of practical operation."[4]

The board did not seem to understand that the brothers were not asking for money for experiments. They were trying to sell a working flying machine. However, since they had not received a patent yet, the brothers refused to reveal publicly how their machine worked, knowing anyone could steal their ideas.

World's First Practical Airplane

By the end of the summer, the Wright brothers had a machine that had flown safely over forty times. The Wright Flyer III of 1905 was the world's first practical airplane. It could fly for several miles. It could make sharp turns. And it could land safely on the ground under full control of the pilot. The Wrights had put the control of the tail rudder back into the hands of the pilot, rather than allowing the rudder to be controlled by its connection to the wing warping system. They had also improved the original gasoline engine.

On October 5, 1905, Wilbur made thirty circles in a flight lasting more than thirty-nine minutes. For the first time, he ran the gasoline tank dry. This record flight was longer than the combined total of all the flights they had taken since the first 1903 flight.

Neighbor Nellie Calhoun remembered that soon afterward, one of the Wright brothers flew over Dayton, circled their Hawthorn Street home, and returned to Huffman Field. The flight had been announced. People came out of their homes and offices to watch. Factory whistles blew. Horns sounded. The Calhouns followed the flight in their 1905 automobile as well as they could.

Because the United States government would not take the Wright brothers' word that their machine could fly, the brothers offered it to European governments. The Wrights had decided not to give the secret of flight to the world for free. They had developed a product. It was their right to sell this product. Therefore, they decided not to fly again until they had made a sale.

However, they encouraged potential customers to talk to local people who had seen their flights. They would not demand payment until the buyer had seen a demonstration and was satisfied. They expected people to believe they were honest. But governments deal with many untrustworthy people. Many of these governments (including the United States) wanted proof first.

European representatives visited Dayton. In March, one French reporter wrote home that, "I have interviewed the witnesses, and it is impossible to doubt the success of their experiments."[5]

In the April 7, 1906, issue of Scientific American, the editors declared that the Wrights deserved the highest credit for perfecting the first heavier-than-air flying machine that could carry a man. This was the first national recognition of their work.

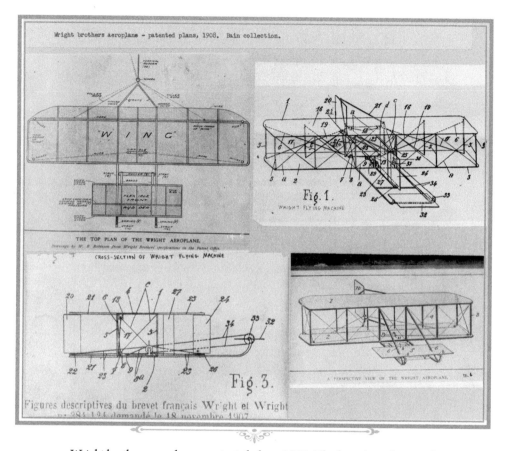

Wright brothers aeroplane—patented plans, 1908. The four plans shown: The top plan is of the Wright Brothers' specification in the Patent Office (top left); Figure 1—Wright flying machine; Figures 3 and 4—figures descriptives de brevet français Wright et Wright (A perspective view of the Wright aeroplane.)

Finally, a Patent

On May 23, 1906, the United States government recognized the Wright brothers' achievement by awarding them a patent for a flying machine: United States Patent number 821,393. It was the broad patent they had wished for, including most of the elements that gave the pilot control of an airplane in flight.

For Sale

Now protected by a patent, the Wrights offered for sale a machine plus patent rights. In addition, the buyer could use the Wright brothers' knowledge, discoveries, formulas, and tables. All this for two hundred thousand dollars.

Groups of buyers talked to them, but hesitated. The Wrights still would not demonstrate their machine in public. They were busy building copies of the one they had for sale to use for demonstrations once they had sold the original.

One newspaper in France wrote an editorial that wondered whether the brothers were flyers or liars? It went on to say, "It is difficult to fly; it is easy to say 'we have flown.'"[6]

On November 12, 1906, another aviator made the news. The first highly advertised public flights in the world were those of Alberto Santos-Dumont near Paris, France. The Brazilian pilot's biplane hopped 726 feet in more than twenty-one seconds. His unstable pusher biplane had the basic design of a box kite. It had been constructed using the little bits of information available in France about the Wright method of flying.

At the same time, a group of Frenchmen was negotiating with the Wrights about buying their flying machine. It was time for the Wrights to go to Europe and demonstrate how to fly.

Chapter 7

THE WRIGHT-CURTISS FEUD BEGINS

G lenn Hammond Curtiss raced motorcycles and manufactured them in Hammondsport, New York. He also sold automobiles. By 1906, all balloonists and gas-bag airships in America used the strong, sturdy, internal-combustion gasoline engines made by the Curtiss factory to operate their propellers.

Curtiss had stopped in Dayton on September 5, 1906. There, he met the Wright brothers and they discussed the problems of flight. The brothers showed him photographs of their earlier Flyers. This chance meeting sparked Curtiss's interest in heavier-than-air flight.

For the next two years, Wilbur and Orville Wright traveled back and forth between Europe and the United States. They shipped a new, improved version of their plane, now called the Type A Flyer, to both France and England. These machines contained seats for two people. All the controls were rods and levers operated by hand instead of the hip cradle. The wing warping and rudder controls were between the two seats and shared by both pilots. In addition, the engine was more powerful.

The Aerial Experiment Association

Meanwhile, a rival group of flight experimenters met in Nova Scotia, Canada. The Aerial Experiment Association (AEA) signed an agreement "for the purpose of constructing a practical aerodrome, driven by its own motive power, and carrying a man."[1]

Alexander Graham Bell, the famous inventor of the telephone, headed the group. His wealthy wife, Mabel, put up the money. Glenn Hammond Curtiss joined as chief engineer. Another partner was army Lieutenant Thomas Selfridge. Bell worked with huge kites that could carry a person. The other members of the group concentrated on building aerodromes—the name given to airplanes in those days.

Possible Sale to the United States

Around Thanksgiving, Wilbur met with officials of the army's Ordnance Department and Signal Corps to discuss the possibility of their buying a Flyer. The Signal Corps published a request for people to submit proposals for selling aircraft to them on December 23.

The airplane the army described in this request was tailored to the current Wright brothers' plane. Forty-one people had submitted proposals for aircraft. Most of these people turned out to be cranks. The two finalists were Augustus Herring and the Wright brothers. In the end, only the Wright brothers were actually able to produce a working Flyer for the trials in 1908. The Wright brothers signed a contract with the United States government on February 8, 1908. A few weeks later, they also signed the French contract they had been negotiating for the past months.

Both contracts required the brothers to demonstrate that their machine could fly. In addition, the machine had to be light enough and strong enough to be transported by horse-drawn wagon.

Around this time, Milton Wright submitted an article for *Who's Who in America*. He described thirty-six-year-old Orville as five feet eight inches tall, weighing one hundred forty pounds. He wrote, "He . . . is very active. His hair is dark and complexion medium. . . . He is excitable, his thoughts quick."

Milton described forty-year-old Wilbur as being the same height and weight. According to Milton, Wilbur was ". . . ready and even rapid in speech, but generally not talkative. . . . he is never rattled in thought or temper."[2]

AEA Flights

Early in 1908, the AEA wrote to the Wright brothers, asking questions ranging from types of material used for wing fabric to the location and effects of air pressure on the wings of planes.

The AEA first tested a plane designed by Selfridge called *Red Wing*. The biplane's wings were arched in a shape called canard. The wings were farther apart in the center and closer together at the ends. It had no lateral control. It crashed in March 1908.

The AEA added three wheels and white fabric and called the new model White Wing. Bell suggested adding small flaps, called ailerons, to the upper wingtips, which would give the plane some lateral control. Bell's idea worked reasonably well. On May 21, Curtiss flew the aircraft 1,017 feet.

The pilot controls used in White Wing and all future planes built by Curtiss were based on his experience with motorcycles. A yoke wrapped around the pilot's shoulders responded to his movements. If the pilot wanted to turn, he would lean in the correct direction. Connecting wires would cause the wings, tail, and ailerons to respond.

Return to Kill Devil Hills

About the same time, the Wright brothers returned to Kill Devil Hills. They practiced flying with a copy of the Type A Flyer Wilbur would be taking to France and Orville would be testing for the Signal Corps. Whenever reporters showed up, the brothers stopped. In desperation, the reporters hid outside the camp among the swamp snakes, mosquito swarms, and ticks to get a glimpse of these secret test flights.

Jimmy Hare of *Collier's* magazine snapped a photograph of the Type A Flyer in flight. It became the first photograph of a Wright brother in a plane to be published in a national magazine.

Byron Newton, a *New York Herald* reporter, described the Flyer making a turn in the air:

> . . . *there was a movement of the forward and rear guiding planes [front elevators and back tail wing], a slight curving of the larger planes [wing] at one end and the machine wheeled at an angle every bit as gracefully as an eagle flying close to the ground could have done.*[3]

The *June Bug*

Back at Hammondsport, New York, the third AEA plane—the *June Bug*—flew 3,430 feet on June 21, 1908. On July 4, Curtiss won the first part of the Scientific American trophy with this plane by flying more than one mile at thirty-nine miles per hour. By this time, many rich people, magazines, and other groups were offering prizes each year to encourage people to fly farther, longer, and higher than before. The Wright brothers refused to enter such competitions. They were preparing their airplane for sale and did not have time to show off.

The AEA flights received a great deal of attention in the newspapers. As Wilbur left for France, he suggested that Orville get an article about their own accomplishments published. Late that summer, Century published what the magazine proudly stated was "the first popular account of their experiments prepared by the inventors."[4]

On July 20, Orville notified Glenn Curtiss that he was infringing on Wright patents. It was the first action of a "patent war" against Curtiss that would last seven years.

Wilbur in France

When the Wrights sent their plane to France, they had arranged for engineers there to build a gasoline engine for it. However, when Wilbur arrived in France, he found that the engine had not been built. In addition, French customs officials at the port of entry had damaged every part of the plane the Wrights had sent. The officials had no idea what these strange items could be. In an effort to detect smuggled goods, they smashed the oil caps, bent the axles, broke the wing ribs, smashed in the seats, and crushed the propeller supports.

Wilbur could only afford his own ticket to France. He had not brought any helpers. Because he did not know enough French to instruct local helpers, he practically rebuilt the plane by himself.

On August 8, Wilbur was ready to demonstrate the Type A Flyer. He flew on the Hunaudières racecourse near LeMans, France. In less than two minutes, he circled the field twice. The crowd was astounded. French planes could only hop short distances. A few could make wide, flat turns. But Wilbur piloted the Type A Flyer around the racecourse, making deep, banking turns.

In England, the August 13 issue of the London Daily Mirror called the Wright brothers' plane "THE MOST WONDERFUL FLYING-MACHINE THAT HAS EVER BEEN MADE!"[5]

Suddenly, the whole world of aeronautics changed. Wilbur Wright had full control of all three axes of flight: pitch, yaw, and roll. The French had seen that the brothers were indeed the first successful flyers.

The country went Wilbur-crazy. The brothers always flew in business suits. Wilbur's only indication of being a pilot was an old, green racing-driver cap—a gift from Orville. Copies of it went on sale in every French city. Every young Frenchman wanted a "Veelbur Reet" cap.[6]

Orville in Virginia

Meanwhile, Orville began the trials for the Army Signal Corps. He arrived at Fort Myer, Virginia, on August 20, 1908. He complained in a letter to Katharine, "I haven't done a lick of work since I have been here. I have to give my time to answering the ten thousand fool questions people ask about the machine."[7]

A committee of five officers judged the Wrights' flying machine. Among them was Lieutenant Thomas Selfridge. The army chose him because of his knowledge of aircraft and his experience with the AEA.

After the first flight, Orville was astonished by the number of people, even experienced reporters, who were moved to tears. Although some of them had heard about the Wright brothers' experiments with flight, this was the first time they had seen it with their very own eyes. The impossible was now a reality—people could fly.

During September, Orville flew every day and set many records. He set a world record for endurance and height: one hour six minutes, flying at two hundred feet. He then proceeded to break this record four times, ending with one hour fourteen minutes at 310 feet.[8] The newspapers kept track of both Wilbur's success in Europe and Orville's records in the United States, announcing when one or the other had broken his brother's record.

Orville took each member of the judging committee up as a passenger. Selfridge waited until last. While waiting, Selfridge tried to pump Orville for information. But behind Orville's back, he constantly criticized the Wright brothers' theories, actions, and skills as pilots and inventors and praised instead the AEA.

Fatal Accident

Finally, Orville and Selfridge took off. Selfridge was the heaviest member of the committee, and it was difficult to get the plane to lift above the grass. After three circles of the parade ground going gradually higher, Orville nosed up to one hundred feet. Suddenly, he heard or felt tapping behind him. There were two thumps, then the plane began to shake violently. The left wing dropped and pulled the nose down. Despite every attempt Orville made to right the machine, they crashed into the ground at top speed.

Both men were pulled bleeding from the wreck. They were carried to the army base hospital on stretchers. There, the doctors discovered Orville had broken his left thigh, plus four ribs. His scalp was bleeding, his back was injured, and he was in shock.

Selfridge's skull had cracked against the frame of the plane. He died after surgery—the very first death in a powered heavier-than-air flying machine. Selfridge's death stopped the trials.

In France, Wilbur blamed himself for the accident. He kept saying, "If I had been there, it would not have happened."[9] He would have insisted that his brother get enough sleep. He would have kept the public from bothering him too much. He would have gone over every part twice to see that it was in good condition. Wilbur canceled all flights and worried about his little brother.

Katharine came as fast as she could to nurse Orville back to health. It was seven weeks before he could be moved back home to Dayton.

Chanute suggested that the accident had been caused by a broken propeller blade. This turned out to be true—the right blade had cracked and flattened. This caused the propellers to work unevenly, which forced the propeller support to give way. The broken blade also clipped a wire holding the rudder. It was the twisted rudder that forced the plane to the ground.

The Army's First Aircraft

At the same time Orville was preparing to demonstrate his heavier-than-air Flyer to the army, the army tested other flying machines. On August 15, 1908, Tom Baldwin successfully piloted his lighter-than-air airship with Glenn Curtiss aboard as the mechanic. The army purchased it. This airship became the United States Army's first aircraft.

Katharine refused to let members of the AEA visit Orville in the hospital. She had heard they had been poking around at the airfield, trying to find some way to blame Orville for the disaster. They had taken measurements of the wing of the Flyer, probably to improve their own planes.

Augustus Herring arrived at the army base with two suitcases and a trunk. He claimed his flying machine was inside but was not quite ready to fly. Since the army had given Orville an extension for his demonstration because of the accident, they would allow Herring one, as well. Herring announced that his machine would fly next year along with Orville's.

By November, Orville was back in Dayton, using a wheelchair. Unfortunately, he never fully recovered from this accident.

Wilbur's Records

Meanwhile, in France, Wilbur broke flying record after flying record. On October 10, he took French physicist Paul Painlevé for a ride that broke distance and duration records for a flight with a passenger. On October 18, he began training Count Charles de Lambert to be the first pilot (other than the Wright brothers) to fly Wright planes. Others clamored to learn.

There were prizes offered by newspaper owners and other groups of millionaires for some of these records to encourage inventors and experimenters to solve the problems of flight.

Wilbur won several gold medals and prizes offered by France, Great Britain, and the United States.

The most prestigious of Wilbur's prizes was the Coupe Michelin prize for longest flight time. On December 31, in a freezing mist, he flew a triangular course for a little over two hours eighteen minutes. He landed when he could no longer stand the cold.

Wilbur moved to the south of France, at Pau, for the winter. Katharine and Orville traveled by ship to join him there. Orville was now walking with two canes.

While at Pau, Wilbur become friends with a boy who had been hanging around the field for days. When Wilbur gave the boy a ride, he was criticized by his business manager. Wilbur responded, "I took up so and so because [I had to]. I took up this boy because I wanted to."[10] This boy was the first child in the world to fly in a heavier-than-air flying machine.

Herring and Curtiss

In the spring of 1909, Augustus Herring formally withdrew from the competition for the Army Signal Corps contract. Instead, he offered the rights to all the patents he claimed to own to Glenn Curtiss. He said his patents for a flying machine predated those of the Wright brothers. Assured by Herring that he had the right to do so, Curtiss began building planes to sell. He did not use the AEA canard-shaped wings. The Herring-Curtiss Company used normal biplane wings, like the Wright brothers' planes.

Europe

In France, Wilbur turned his plane over to the people he had hired to oversee sales in that country. He then trained Italian pilots and turned the plane over to his Italian representatives.

On April 24, 1909, Wilbur took a Universal Newsreel cameraman aloft. The cameraman took motion pictures from the viewpoint of a passenger in an airplane for the very first time.

Now people who would never be able to fly could still experience the breathtaking views. Milton Wright was able to see this newsreel in a Dayton movie theater. It was the first time he experienced what his sons did high up in the air.

Celebration at Home

The Wright brothers returned to America in early May 1909. They were now international celebrities. Newspaper editors who had refused to print articles about their work because they thought the brothers were crackpots now gave them front-page coverage. Ten thousand people welcomed Wilbur, Orville, and Katharine at the train depot in Dayton, Ohio, on May 13. Others gathered at their Hawthorn Street home, lighting the street with Chinese lanterns and electric lights.

The brothers avoided the Dayton parties. They were preparing for the next round of army air trials. When they visited Washington, D.C., on June 9, they had to divide their time between business meetings and the celebrations planned for them.

They returned to Dayton for the Wright Brothers' Home Days Celebration on June 17 and 18. Wilbur wrote to Chanute:

> About a week of the time will be consumed in traveling back and forth between Dayton and Washington to receive medals. The Dayton presentation has been made the excuse for an elaborate carnival and advertisement of the city under the guise of being an honor to us. As it was done in spite of our known wishes, we are not as appreciative as we might be.[11]

Chanute advised these two shy, private men to accept the fact that they were now celebrated heroes.

The Home Days Celebration included band concerts, receptions, and a carnival. Evening fireworks featured a United States flag plus portraits of Wilbur and Orville in fireworks eight feet tall. On June 18, the two brothers, each in a swallowtail coat and tall silk top hat, received the Congressional Medal of Honor,

Ohio State gold medals, and the City of Dayton medal, sparkling with diamonds. The ceremony ended with a singing, living flag—made up of schoolchildren dressed in red, white, and blue.

Curtiss Airplanes

Though the Wrights were now famous, they still had problems. Glenn Hammond Curtiss sold his first Curtiss airplane, the Golden Flyer, to the Aeronautic Society of New York on June 26, 1909. Included in the Wright brothers' broad patent were the ailerons placed on the back edge of the wing. To avoid infringing on the Wright brothers' patent, Curtiss mounted his ailerons between the wings on the struts. In addition, his plane was a single seater with the seat in front of the wings, not on them.

Sale to the United States

The Wright brothers spent July running tests at Fort Myer, Virginia. Despite his pain from the 1908 crash, Orville did all the flying. He was determined to finish the job he had begun. For the final demonstration on July 30, he flew a speed trial (to see how fast the plane could safely go) with a passenger—Lieutenant Benjamin Foulois—who had helped them put the Flyer together.

Their speed had been 42.583 miles per hour. This was 2.583 miles per hour faster than needed to fulfill the requirements for the sale of a heavier-than-air flying machine to the United States Army Signal Corp. That meant they would receive a bonus. On August 2, they were paid thirty thousand dollars.

Now they could concentrate on protecting their patent. Curtiss had ignored their warnings. He had refused to pay for the right to use their inventions on his aircraft. The brothers began a long court battle with Curtiss for his infringement of the Wright brothers' patent on flight.[12]

Chapter 8

THE PATENT WAR

In August 1909, Katharine and Orville Wright traveled to Germany to promote the sale of their plane. Wilbur went to New York State to file a bill of complaint to stop Glenn Hammond Curtiss and the Herring-Curtiss Company from manufacturing, selling, or exhibiting airplanes. He then filed other suits in New York City.

However, Curtiss was in Reims, France, becoming the fastest man in the air. In a contest the Wright brothers had refused (as usual) to enter, all the records Wilbur had set in 1908 were broken. Curtiss flew two laps of the course at 47.1 miles per hour on Saturday, August 28.

Back in the states, the Wright brothers' lawyers argued that both Herring and Curtiss had had opportunities to observe the Wrights' patented flight techniques. Curtiss and Herring countered that their mid-wing ailerons were new—and not covered by the Wright brothers' patents.

Germany

In Germany, Orville was welcomed by crowds and by the German emperor, Kaiser Wilhelm II. Between August 30 and October 4, Orville recaptured the world records for length of flight with a passenger and for altitude.

On October 2, Crown Prince Friedrich Wilhelm flew with Orville sixteen hundred feet in the air. In appreciation, he took off a stickpin he had been wearing and gave it to Orville. It was a crown set in rubies with a W in diamonds. He pointed out that although the W actually stood for Wilhelm, it could also stand for Wright.

Hudson-Fulton Celebration

At the same time, New York City held the huge Hudson-Fulton Celebration, honoring both the three-hundredth anniversary of Henry Hudson's entry into New York Harbor and Robert Fulton's first use of a steamboat on the Hudson River. The city invited both Curtiss and Wilbur Wright to fly around the harbor. The two men met face to face. They ignored the patent dispute. They casually talked about Curtiss's adventures at Reims, France.

However, when it came time to fly upriver, Curtiss's small plane could not handle the winds rushing down the river valley. He had been paid to be at the celebration for only one week. At the week's end, the winds were still strong. Curtiss left without having flown.

On Monday, October 4, Wilbur took off. He used a standard Wright Flyer with one addition. He strapped a sealed red canoe beneath the plane—just in case he had to land the plane in the water.

More than a million people saw him fly the round-trip of twenty-one miles from Governors Island in New York Harbor, up the Hudson River to Grant's tomb in the northern part of New York City, and back. Two American flags fluttered from the front of the plane. The entire flight took only a little over thirty-three minutes. The crowds held their breath when Wilbur flew over factory smokestacks. The hot gasses coming out of the stacks made the plane swoop in dangerous-looking plunges, but Wilbur kept full control.

At the end of the day, Wilbur told a reporter that this would be the last public flight either of the Wrights would make. Any other flights would simply be to test new improvements to their planes.

The Wright Company

Lorin Wright, a professional bookkeeper, had been handling the family accounts. Millions of dollars came in from the sale of planes and patent rights in different countries. More came from prizes the brothers had won. It all got to be too complicated.

On November 22, 1909, the Wright Company was incorporated. Wilbur was elected president. Shy Orville refused to participate in running the company, even though he was vice president. The board of directors was made up of many important businessmen who had invested in the company, including millionaire Cornelius Vanderbilt; Robert Collier, owner of Collier's Weekly magazine; and Russell Alger of the Packard Motor Car Company. The two bicycle-shop owners of Dayton, Ohio, were now rubbing shoulders with the elite in the business world. The company's offices were located in New York City, with a factory in Dayton.

This new company purchased the Wright brothers' patent rights and the experienced advice of the brothers. In exchange, the brothers received one third of the total shares in the new company, plus a 10 percent royalty on every airplane sold. This company would continue to prosecute patent infringers.

Late that year, Augustus Herring was asked by the board of directors of the Herring-Curtiss Company to produce his own patents of airplane invention. The patents were needed to fight the Wright patent suit. Herring had no patents—only a rejected application for one. This crisis caused the Herring-Curtiss Company to file for bankruptcy.

The Wrights wanted their new company to handle the business and allow them to get back to research. However, this did not work out as well as they had hoped. As president of the company, Wilbur's time was taken up attending meetings and making speeches.

Stopping Curtiss

On January 3, 1910, their injunction against Curtiss was granted by the Federal Circuit Court in Buffalo, New York. Curtiss was ordered to stop making and selling airplanes. The Wright brothers served notice to all the people using the brothers' results of many years of plane-building experiments, that the brothers wanted credit for being first. They got an angry letter from Octave Chanute saying, ". . . your usually sound judgment has been warped by the desire for great wealth."[1]

Wilbur wrote back on January 29, replying that anyone who knew the Wright family well would never accuse them of wanting wealth. The two brothers had tried for several years to get enough money back from their invention to allow them to live modestly and to support their research. During most of the previous years, they had lived off the income from the bicycle shop.

Unfortunately, none of their efforts to make their invention pay had worked. Therefore, the Wright brothers had been forced to go to court to enforce what they considered their rights. Wilbur explained to Chanute that, "We honestly think that our work of 1900–1906 has been and will be of value to the world, and that the world owes us something as inventors, regardless of whether we personally make [a big show] for accident-loving crowds."[2]

Anger over the accusations caused the Wrights' friendship with Chanute to come to an end.

Air Exhibitions

Curtiss was already making money performing for crowds. People flocked to air exhibitions. There, they could watch a miracle—a flying man. One of the ways Curtiss fought the Wright brothers' court orders was by changing the method used to steer his own planes. Whereas the Wright brothers used upright rods on either side of the pilot, Curtiss's machines used a wheel similar to a car's.

When the Wright brothers created their two-seater plane, the steering sticks to the outside left of one pilot and to the outside right of the other pilot controlled the same area of the plane. The control stick between the two pilots was shared. Wright pilots learned to be either "left-seat" or "right-seat" pilots. Curtiss's single control-wheel column pivoted either in front of one pilot or the other.

The Wright Company opened a flying school near Montgomery, Alabama. Another flying school was begun at Huffman Field on March 24, 1910. It was still a cow pasture that turned muddy when it rained. The thorn tree at one end threatened unwary flyers. Flyers who were trained here learned to handle adverse flying conditions. Curtiss opened his own flying school in California.

Wright pilots trained under strict rules—the same rules that governed the Wright family. There would be no drinking, no gambling, and no flying on Sundays. That first year, the Wright Exhibition Team brought in one hundred thousand dollars.

"Hap" Arnold, a Wright flyer, said, "The crowd . . . gaped at the wonders, the exhibits of planes from home and abroad, secure in the knowledge that nowhere on earth . . . was there such a good chance of seeing somebody break their neck."[3]

On May 25, 1910, the two brothers broke their rule about never flying together in the same plane. Flying together, they demonstrated to their proud father all the things a plane could do.

Henry "Hap" Arnold

Lieutenant Henry "Hap" Arnold was one of the 115 Wright pilots trained at Huffman Field. He later became a five-star general, commanding the United States Army Air Force in World War II.

Then they invited eighty-two-year-old Bishop Milton Wright aboard for a six-minute flight. Orville was very careful not to fly higher than 350 feet, but his father kept yelling with joy, "Higher, Orville. Higher!"[4]

The Patent Case Drags On

On June 14, 1910, Curtiss's lawyers won their appeal against the injunction. The court of appeals removed the injunction against the Herring-Curtiss Company. Curtiss was free to do business until the court case was finally settled.

With the patent wars, the world's view of the Wright brothers changed. Earlier, they had been considered naive, odd geniuses. They had puzzled the French. These men did not smoke, drink, gamble, or flirt with women. Americans had been proud of the Wrights. The brothers had proved that hard work and strong family values could achieve miracles.

Now the whole world saw the Wrights claiming a monopoly on aeronautical information. They saw the Wrights as greedy men who were threatening to slow down the development of flight.

The Model B

A new plane, the Wright Model B aircraft, was built on June 29, 1910. This plane had wheels mounted on its skids and did not need to be launched from a derrick. In addition, the elevator was now placed in the rear of the plane.

Then on November 7, the Wrights demonstrated that the airplane could have a commercial use. Orville and Katharine strapped two bolts of dress silk onto the passenger seat of a Model B at Huffman Field. When it arrived sixty-five miles away in Columbus, Ohio, an automobile delivered the silk to the Morehouse-Martens Department Store. The world's first air-freight shipment took only one hour six minutes. It was faster than either a train or a car at that time. However, it was not practical yet; wagon and train cars could carry larger quantities of goods.

Orville wrote, "I cannot but believe that we stand at the beginning of a new era, the Age of Flight. . . ."[5]

Although flying was becoming extremely successful, more air exhibit pilots were being injured in accidents. Each air exhibit pilot tried to do more dangerous tricks to scare the crowd. On November 17, 1910, Ralph Johnstone, one of the foremost air daredevils, spiraled down, smashing into the ground. He was the first American pilot, as opposed to a passenger, to die in an air crash.

Octave Chanute Dies

Another death saddened the world of aeronautics. Octave Chanute died on November 23, 1910, after a long illness. Before he died, he and Wilbur talked about preserving their correspondence for future historians. Both his letters and the Wright brothers' letters were published in separate books in the 1950s.

Flight Simulator

The Wright system of flying, using both hands on levers, was difficult to learn. To help pilots, Orville created the world's first flight simulator. He simply placed an old plane on sawhorses. It was balanced so that it could tip from side to side. Pulling on the correct lever allowed the student to keep the plane level.

Transcontinental Flight

On September 17, 1911, Calbraith Rodgers, a Wright pilot, began the first transcontinental flight. He took off from Sheepshead Bay, Long Island, New York, in a new Wright model EX single-seater biplane called the Vin Fiz.

The Hearst newspaper company had offered a prize of $50,000 to the first person to fly across the United States in thirty days. Despite the special train following him with spare parts, Rodgers did not reach Long Beach, California, until December 10, 1911. He had to stop frequently to repair his plane and recover from injuries from eleven accidents.

In November, the Wrights disbanded their exhibition teams. Both the Wrights and Curtiss spoke out against all the fancy flying that occasionally resulted in the death of the pilot and sometimes members of the audience.

Chapter 9

LIFE AFTER WILBUR

In February 1912, the Wright family bought seventeen acres of land high on a hill overlooking Dayton. Helped by an architect, Orville designed a mansion for the site, which they called Hawthorn Hill.

Orville involved himself in all parts of the building decisions—from designing the plumbing, heating, and electrical systems to choosing rugs. Rainwater collected in cisterns on the roof was used for bathwater because it was free of minerals. The shower was a set of circular pipes that surrounded a person from shoulder to knees. He also built a vacuum system into the walls.

Meanwhile, during the winter of 1911 and 1912, Wilbur testified at the trial for the Curtiss infringement of the Wright patents. Shy Orville continued to let his brother be the speaker for the two of them. People were impressed with the clear way Wilbur presented evidence.

The traveling and presentations were extremely hard on Wilbur's health, though. He always returned from trips to New York City courts pale and tired. Thus, his immune system was weak when he ate shellfish on a trip to Boston in late April 1912. Shellfish that comes from polluted water can carry disease. Wilbur came down with typhoid.

He felt well enough to return to Dayton on May 2, but then got worse. On May 10, he wrote his will. He still joked with his nieces and nephews when they visited him but he tired quickly. Wilbur slowly faded away. He died on May 30, 1912, at 3:15 A.M. He was forty-five years old.

Thousands of telegrams flooded Dayton. Enough flowers arrived to fill a train boxcar. Newspapers all over the country paid tribute to Wilbur.

The Wright family was not able to have a quiet family funeral. Twenty-five thousand people viewed Wilbur's coffin at the First Presbyterian Church. At 3:30 P.M. on Sunday, June 1, all activity in Dayton paused as people mourned Wilbur Wright.

Bishop Wright wrote in his diary on June 3 that the whole family was upset, but that Orville and Katharine felt Wilbur's loss the most. The daily humor of the family stopped. Many months passed before Orville felt up to joking or playing practical jokes.

Orville's Quiet Depression

For a while, Orville lost interest in work. He spent most of his time in 1912 and early 1913 with his nieces and nephews. He built a sled for them, using airplane skids for runners. He also took them on automobile trips, teaching them about the plants and animals they saw.

And then at one Sunday dinner, Orville teased his nephew Bus about his love of mashed potatoes. Suddenly, Bus's plate moved toward the bowl of mashed potatoes in the center of the table. Everyone screamed—mostly with laughter. Uncle Orv had glued a white thread to the bottom of Bus's plate. Sitting across the table from Bus, he had pulled the plate until it crashed into the mashed potatoes.

Flood

The Great Miami River is joined by the Stillwater and Mad rivers at Dayton. These three rivers flooded the city on March 25, 1913. Eight feet of water swept over Hawthorn Street. The family found shelter at friends' homes.

Upon returning, they discovered that all of their photographic equipment, including the glass plate negatives, were covered with water and mud. These included not only family pictures but also the photographic record of all the Wright brothers' air experiments.

The negative of the first flight in 1903, however, had been only slightly damaged in one corner. Their written records were completely safe. These had been stored on a second floor, where the water never reached them.

The boxes containing the pieces of the 1903 plane had been covered under twelve feet of water in the back of the bicycle shop. The Wrights simply scraped off the thick layer of mud and restacked the boxes.

President of the Company

After Wilbur's death, Orville took his brother's place as president of the Wright Company. But he was not suited for the job. Where Wilbur was ambitious and had a drive to succeed, Orville was quiet and withdrawn. He was uncomfortable making speeches and presiding over company meetings. The businessmen in New York City who ran the Wright Company had been Wilbur's friends, not Orville's. Orville stayed in Dayton, working in his lab above the bicycle shop. The back pain caused by the air accident at Fort Myer in 1908 became worse over the years, preventing him from doing much traveling.

Orville also inherited his brother's secretary, Mabel Beck. For the rest of his life, Beck protected him from the rest of humanity. She was rude and abrasive to people who wanted to contact Orville, but no one dared to offend her. She was the only one who could give them permission to speak to Orville Wright. He valued her protection.

He hired Grover Loening, one of the first aeronautical engineers, to manage the Dayton factory. Eventually, they became good friends. Orville bounced ideas for inventions off Loening's agile mind and argued with him aggressively. Loening decided that Orville missed his arguments with Wilbur. He said, "Many a night I had to do extra thinking and studying to be prepared to meet Orville's clear, pungent and devastatingly correct points the next day . . . he would remember every word I'd used the day before."[1]

Another Invention

Meanwhile, the Wright Model C plane turned out to be tail heavy and unstable. It caused crashes and several pilot deaths. Orville barricaded himself in his workshop for several weeks perfecting an automatic stabilization system that cured the problem. It was patented in October.

Loening encouraged Orville to submit this device for the 1913 Robert J. Collier Trophy offered by the Aero Club of America for the "Greatest Achievement in Aviation, demonstrated during that year." It was the demonstration that was the hard part. Shy Orville did not like to fly in public. It meant he would have to speak to the observers. Loening kept urging him. Finally, Orville gave in and entered.

Orville flew, as usual, in business clothing. On the field, he limped less, smiled more, and barked orders with energy. In the air, he was calm, precise, and comfortably at home—in full command of his ship.

On a cold December day with snow in the air, Orville began the demonstration. Once, twice, many times he flew in front of the group of observers. He flew close to the ground, sitting with his arms off the controls. The plane plowed steadily on, despite gusts of wind, making perfect turns. It was easily the greatest aviation achievement of 1913. Orville won the Collier Trophy.

Things had piled up because of Wilbur's death. Orville was aware that he should write and publish detailed reports of their experiments with flight, especially those at Kill Devil Hills, but he could not bring himself to begin. Wilbur had been the writer in the family. Orville tended to focus on the technology, not information about their private life. Eventually, he did write a few articles for publication.

In February 1914, the Army Board of Investigations declared pusher planes too dangerous and grounded them all. A newer, better plane with propellers in front, called a tractor design, had become more popular, and it was safer. Now the Wright Factory was forced to design tractor planes or go out of business.

The chief engineer of the Dayton factory, Grover Loening, headed this Army Board of Investigations. He was absolutely fair in his judgment. He did not avoid making this ruling—which effectively ruined the production of Wright pusher planes—just because he worked for the Wright factory.

A Newer and Better Automatic Stabilizer

Orville did not remain the only inventor of an automatic stabilizer for long. Lawrence Sperry, a pilot for Curtiss, wondered if the invention his father, Elmer Sperry, had created—a gyroscope to stabilize ships—would work for planes. In California on June 18, 1914, Sperry used two gyroscopes in an airplane. One sensed the yaw and operated the rudder. The other sensed the roll and the pitch and controlled the ailerons and the elevator. The gyroscope, not Orville's invention, became the basis for all automatic stability systems thereafter. It is now called an automatic pilot.

Hawthorn Hill

On April 4, 1914, Orville, Katharine, and Milton Wright moved into their new house on Hawthorn Hill. They could afford it. Because of the court rulings in the patent suits, all plane manufacturers in the United States had been paying the Wrights a 20 percent royalty on every plane they produced for the past few years. This added up to a lot of money.

The Great Aerodrome Rises Again

The Smithsonian had acknowledged that the Wright brothers were the first to fly a heavier-than-air machine. However, they still had pieces of Samuel Pierpont Langley's Great Aerodrome. The Smithsonian gave Curtiss money to test it again to prove it was capable of flight.

Curtiss corrected the original faults of the Great Aerodrome. He launched it from the surface of Lake Keuka near Hammondsport, New York, on May 28, 1914. It flew one hundred fifty feet. Curtiss tweaked it a bit more, added an engine of his own design, and made more flights.

The 1914 and 1915 Smithsonian Annual Reports claimed that Curtiss flew Langley's Great Aerodrome without any changes. This infuriated the Wright family. The Great Aerodrome as designed by Langley did not and was not able to fly. The wings were not designed correctly to lift off.

Lorin Wright had observed parts of the test. Even the photographs released by the Smithsonian showed the improvements Curtiss had made—mainly to the wing arrangement of wires and structure.

However, for years afterward, the Smithsonian displayed the Langley Aerodrome with the sign: "The first man-carrying aeroplane in the history of the world capable of sustained free flight."[2] This meant that a head of the Smithsonian, with the support of the United States government behind him, was the first person to design a capable flying machine—not those bicycle-shop owners from Dayton, Ohio. The Wrights' feud with the Smithsonian lasted for almost thirty years.

World War I Begins

World War I began the summer of 1914 in Europe. Beginning with Germany and Austria fighting England, France, Italy, and Russia, it soon involved almost every country in Europe, as well as others around the world. The war broke out as a result of years of hostility over economics, colonialism, and a buildup of arms. Unfortunately, both sides were almost equal in strength. Neither side could claim a quick victory. The war dragged on.

The United States did not enter the war at first. It remained neutral. In Ohio, Orville wanted to return to research and invention. He sold the Wright Company to a group of men headed by mining tycoon William Boyce Thompson. This sale made Orville a wealthy man. The amount he was paid for the company was never revealed, but it may have been more than $1.5 million.[3]

Back home, he worked with the Dayton Engineer Laboratories (DELCO). He and his friends Charles F. Kettering, Edward A. Deeds, and the Harold Talbotts, father and son, had formed DELCO in 1914 to produce an automobile self-starter that Kettering had invented. This device, which enabled the driver to start an automobile with a key from the driver's seat instead of a crank inserted into the engine at the front of the automobile, became widely popular. Now the group worked on developing other helpful inventions.

A Summer Home

In 1916, Orville bought rocky Lambert Island in Lake Huron from Canada. There, he puttered about the twenty acres of land every summer for thirty-two years, making improvements to his original purchase.

The main house on Lambert Island was at the top of the one-hundred-foot-tall rocky hill and had a view over the lake for miles around. There were also several guest cottages in rocky glens.

Supplies were taken up to the cottages by Orville's little railroad. It was a flatbed car that ran on a small wooden track and was pulled up the hill by a cable. The outside end of the train car was raised, which made the surface flat as it traveled up the hill. Orville was the only person who could run the motor driving the cable. He had taken the motor from an old outboard boat engine.

There was no electricity on the island. Water for drinking and bathing came from the bay. It was pumped to the water tower by a small gasoline motor, which seemed to work properly only if Orville was there to fiddle with it. (Many of Orville's home improvements here and at Hawthorn Hill worked only when he could be there to tinker with them.) One line of water pipes went through the icebox, creating a constant supply of cool drinking water.

Orville also created a rinsing machine. (Modern washing machines had not been perfected yet.) First, the clothes were washed by hand. Then, they were placed into a metal tub set at an angle. When the water pump down at the lake was started, the person standing by the rinsing tub aimed the water hose at it. The tub would spin, flinging all the soapy water out of the tub. In this way, the clothes would be rinsed and then spun until they were barely damp.

Orville made a toaster out of two sheets of metal that could be used on a coal stove. It made toast that was dry, hard, smooth, and tasty. He invented a special device to slice bread exactly the right thickness for his toaster. Friends and family ate the toast with Orville's homemade marmalade.

Orville made the stove that warmed the main house during cool nights out of a small oil drum and stove pipe. In it, he could burn newspapers and small pieces of wood.

Changes in Family Life

Sometime in March 1917, Orville brought home a fluffy sixteen-pound Saint Bernard puppy. Orville named him Scipio, but Katharine called the dog Baby.

Just after the addition of this new "family member," the Wrights lost another family member. Bishop Milton Wright died in his sleep on April 3, 1917. He was eighty-nine years old. After their father died, Orville and Katharine remained together, living at Hawthorn Hill.

The Wright Business

The original Wright Company, which Orville had sold in 1914, merged with the Glenn Martin Company to create the Wright-Martin Corporation in 1916. This company made airplane motors to be used in World War I. Almost one thousand motors were produced and delivered before the war.

Orville still owned the Wright Company factory in Dayton, however. His friend Colonel Edward Deeds was appointed to be on the government committee that chose companies to manufacture equipment for the armed forces. He convinced the committee to award the Dayton-Wright Company factory a contract to produce forty-four hundred aircraft for World War I—thus ensuring that the people of Dayton would have jobs.

The factory made a variation of an airplane called the British DeHavilland 4. In Dayton, it was called the DH-4. Orville's niece Ivonette's fiancé, Harold Miller, later told Orville that the airmen of World War I were afraid to fly the DH-4. The airmen nicknamed the DH-4 the "flaming coffin," because of its large, unprotected gas tank.[4] Not many of these planes reached the front before the war ended.

The United States entered World War I in 1917. Americans had become upset by German submarine attacks on unarmed passenger ships and hoped to help defeat the Central Powers by getting involved in the war. Orville was in favor of using American planes to keep enemy planes from observing the Allied troop movements: ". . . the supremacy in the air must be so complete as to entirely blind the enemy."[5]

During the time the United States was involved in World War I, Orville developed a code machine that made it possible for the American forces to pass messages without the enemy understanding them.

Orville Wright flew for the last time on May 13, 1918, in a 1911 Wright biplane. He flew in formation with the first Dayton-built DH-4s.

Near the end of the war, Orville wrote that he had no regrets about inventing planes, which could be used to shoot, bomb, and kill. He wrote, "The Aeroplane has made war so terrible that I do not believe any country will again care to start a war."[6]

The 1920s

After World War I ended in 1918 with an Allied victory, in January 1920, President Woodrow Wilson appointed Orville to the National Advisory Committee for Aeronautics. It worked to identify research that would help the development of flight—like the automatic pilot stabilizer Orville Wright himself had worked on. Among the committee members was soon-to-be-famous aviator Charles Lindbergh. He and Orville became close friends.

Inventions

Orville always invited relatives and their wives and children to spend time with him and Katharine at Hawthorn Hill. He made them feel at home with his teasing and joking—and by sharing his inventions.

At Christmas at Hawthorn Hill in 1923, Orville showed off a toy he had created called Flips and Flops. On it, a clown on a trapeze caught another clown when it was released from a spring. Then both clowns made the trapeze revolve. The toy sold well. The toy's patent was the last one granted to him. Orville's next toy was a small Wright Flyer. Businesses could print advertising

Solo Flight

Charles A. Lindbergh became famous in 1927, when he became the first man to fly alone, nonstop, from Long Island, New York, across the Atlantic Ocean to Paris, France. He flew thirty-six hundred miles in thirty-three and a half hours in a small plane called the Spirit of St. Louis. It was driven by a Wright motor. On his way home from this flight, Lindbergh stopped at Dayton, Ohio, to visit Orville Wright.

on its wings and give it away to customers. He did not bother to apply for a patent for it.

Katharine Leaves

On November 20, 1926, fifty-three-year-old Katharine Wright married Henry J. Haskell, an old Oberlin College friend. Orville's emotional security was shattered.[7] Orville was dependent on his sister and was extremely hurt that she was leaving him alone. Orville resolved to never talk to her or communicate with her ever again. The Haskells moved to Kansas City, where Haskell was the editor of the Kansas City Star.

In the spring of 1928, Orville learned that Katharine was ill with pneumonia. Despite Orville's vow never to speak to her again, brother Lorin insisted that Orville go with him to see her. They arrived in time to sit by her side when she died on March 3, 1929.

New Home for the Flyer

Many organizations requested permission to display the 1903 Flyer. The Smithsonian did not want the plane. It was a rival to Langley's Great Aerodrome, which they already had on display.

Therefore, in January 1928, Orville granted the request of the Science Museum of London, England, to display the 1903

Flyer. Suddenly, the American public became aware that one of their national treasures was no longer in the United States. Orville Wright sat back and let the public protests influence the Smithsonian.

Two Rival Companies Merge

In 1929, the Wright-Curtiss feud finally was laid to rest. The old Wright Company, now called Wright Aeronautical, merged with Curtiss Aeroplane and Motor. The two rivals had become one. The Curtiss-Wright Corporation became the second-largest manufacturer of aircraft and engines.

Monuments

In the 1920s and 1930s, monuments to the Wright brothers were built at every place in the United States they had flown, the first at the Outer Banks in 1927. In 1932, Orville and his relatives attended the dedication of the Wright Memorial Monument in North Carolina. The sixty-foot-high granite shaft had been built on top of ninety-foot-high Big Kill Devil Hill.

For this ceremony, on November 19, 1932, everyone drove over the new Wright Memorial Bridge, which connected the island to the mainland. This was the first and only time a living person was at the ceremony dedicating a monument to him.

Also during the 1930s, automobile manufacturer Henry Ford gathered historic buildings from around the United States and set them up in historic Greenfield Village, near Dearborn, Michigan. In 1937, Ford moved one of the Wright brothers' bicycle shops, plus the Hawthorn Street house, to the village. These new additions were dedicated on April 16, 1938—Wilbur Wright's birthday.

On Orville's sixty-ninth birthday, August 19, 1940, Dayton dedicated its own monument to the Wright brothers. It stands on a hill on Wright-Patterson Air Force Base, overlooking the Huffman flying field. Army General "Hap" Arnold was the main speaker. Dr. Charles Greeley Abbot, secretary of the Smithsonian, who had come to honor the Wrights, was embarrassed to hear speakers criticize the fact that the 1903 plane was still in London.

The End of the Smithsonian Feud

Fred C. Kelly, a reporter and friend of Orville Wright's, decided to do something about the Smithsonian feud with the Wrights. He was in the middle of writing a biography of the Wright brothers when Orville asked him to stop. Orville did not want personal information about the Wright family being published. Kelly thought that if he could do something to please the Wright family, he might be allowed to finish the book.

He negotiated with the Smithsonian. The Wright family wanted the Smithsonian to publish an article pointing out the differences between the 1903 Aerodrome and the one Curtiss flew in 1914. In addition, the Smithsonian would have to reconfirm that the Wright brothers' 1903 Flyer was the only one capable of flight at that time.

Kelly asked secretary of the Smithsonian Charles Abbot to write an article confessing to thirty-five changes in the Aerodrome. Abbot, also wanting to end the feud, agreed. The article was published in Smithsonian Miscellaneous Collections magazine on October 24, 1942.

Orville Wright, pleased with this gesture, began taking steps to move the Flyer back to the United States. Orville appreciated Kelly's work in resolving the Smithsonian feud and approved Kelly's manuscript. *The Wright Brothers: A Biography Authorized by Orville Wright* was published on May 13, 1943. It is full of the humor and charm of the Wright family.

Silent Orville

The year 1943 was the fortieth anniversary of the first flight by Wilbur and Orville Wright. Orville agreed to attend a special dinner in Washington, D.C.—on the condition that he not be asked to give a speech. His overwhelming shyness in public still made him uncomfortable.

The fact that the 1903 plane would be returning to the United States was to be announced by President Franklin Roosevelt at this dinner. However, when Orville arrived, he was told that the president would not be able to attend. Instead, Roosevelt wanted Orville to present the Collier Trophy to General "Hap" Arnold.

Because Orville and Arnold were friends, the organizers thought Orville would enjoy this. They were wrong. Orville was furious. He thought everyone understood that he never spoke in public.

During the ceremony, Orville stood up, handed the trophy to Arnold, and sat down again—in silence. The ceremony was being recorded by newsreel cameras and was broadcast on radio. Eventually, the radio announcer filled the silence by announcing that Orville Wright had handed the Collier Trophy to General Arnold. Arnold helped cover the awkward moment by saying that there was no one from whom he would rather receive the trophy than Orville Wright.[8]

Because of this embarrassment, Orville refused to allow the return of the plane to be announced before his death.

Chapter 10

THE FINAL
RECOGNITION

W orld War II, which began in 1939 with Germany's invasion of Poland and came to involve almost every country in Europe as well as the United States and Japan, ended on September 2, 1945. Orville Wright, in the meantime, continued to tinker with his own inventions and to try to understand new advances, such as the electric typewriter.

Heart Attacks

Orville had his first heart attack on the steps of the National Cash Register Company on October 10, 1947. He had been rushing to a meeting with Edward Deeds. At the hospital, when he was not teasing the nurses, he was trying to figure out how to improve the efficiency and comfort of the oxygen tent.

The next year, he spent the morning of January 27, 1948, tinkering with the doorbell of Hawthorn Hill. When he arrived at his lab, he had a second heart attack. At the Miami Valley Hospital, he teased the nurses that this was the only way he could think of to see them again. He died at 10:30 P.M. on January 30 at the age of seventy-seven.

To honor Orville Wright, Dayton held a huge public funeral on February 2. Four jet fighters circled Dayton as Orville Wright's body was carried to Woodland Cemetery. Flags flew at half-mast throughout the United States. Dayton schoolchildren were dismissed at noon.

Orville Wright left an estate worth more than a million dollars. The Library of Congress took all the Wright brothers' letters, notebooks, scrapbooks, and photographs that pertained to flight to store in the nation's library.

Legends in Their Own Time

The Wright brothers had become legends. They had been given awards and medals. These men, who had not even received high school diplomas, had received eleven honorary degrees from American and European colleges and universities.

Some people called the Wright brothers ordinary men, with no special advantages, who managed to figure out how to fly. Orville Wright disagreed. He insisted that he and Wilbur had been given very special advantages: "If my father had not been the kind who encouraged his children to pursue intellectual interests without any thought of profit, our early curiosity about flying would have been nipped too early to bear fruit."[1]

The Flyer on the Moon

In 1969, astronaut Neil Armstrong, a member of the historic group of Americans to first land on and explore the surface of the moon, carried a piece of the original wing fabric from the Wrights' 1903 Flyer when he stepped out of the spacecraft to walk on the moon.

Wilbur always saw the big picture. He was the visionary. Orville was a born engineer who concentrated on the details that made Wilbur's ideas work. Together, they made a formidable team. Their father told people that they worked as closely together as twins.

The Flyer Returns to the United States

What was to become of the 1903 airplane, which was still in England at the time of Orville Wright's death? Reporters badgered the family. When Orville's will was read, the world learned of Orville's request to send the plane to the Smithsonian.

This was successfully done during the fall of 1948. Navy trucks delivering the 1903 Wright Flyer carried big signs that read, "Operation Homecoming." Charles Lindbergh's Spirit of St. Louis was moved to make room for the Flyer. Lindbergh said it would be an honor to share the same exhibit hall.

A grand celebration occurred when the Flyer was finally hung in the Smithsonian Institution in Washington, D.C. Ceremonies were held in the Smithsonian Arts and Industries Building on December 17, 1948—the forty-fifth anniversary of the first powered, sustained, and controlled flight. The 1903 Wright Flyer seemed to fly over the heads of the huge audience.

A sign announced:

BY ORIGINAL SCIENTIFIC RESEARCH THE WRIGHT BROTHERS DISCOVERED THE PRINCIPLES OF HUMAN FLIGHT AS INVENTORS, BUILDERS, AND FLYERS THEY FURTHER DEVELOPED THE AEROPLANE, TAUGHT MAN TO FLY, AND OPENED THE ERA OF AVIATION[2]

In 1976, in time for the bicentennial of the United States, the new Smithsonian National Air and Space Museum building opened. The 1903 Wright Flyer now hangs in a place of honor over the entrance from the mall.

The Wright brothers' official biographer, Fred Kelly, once asked Orville if the biggest "kick" out of the invention of flight was the moment the machine actually took off in 1903.[3]

"No," Orville said, "I got more thrill out of flying before I had ever been in the air at all—while lying in bed thinking how exciting it would be to fly."[4]

CHRONOLOGY

1867—Wilbur Wright is born on April 16.

1871—Orville Wright is born on August 19.

1889—Orville begins publishing the weekly Dayton newspaper West Side News.

1893—The Wright brothers open a bicycle shop.

1896—Orville Wright almost dies of typhoid; The brothers learn of the death of Otto Lilienthal and begin their study of flight.

1899—Wilbur writes to the Smithsonian Institution; Wilbur discovers wing warping for lateral control; The brothers build and test a biplane kite.

1900—The Wrights conduct their first flights of a kite-glider on the Outer Banks near Kitty Hawk in September and October.

1901—The Wrights return to Kitty Hawk and Kill Devil Hills in July; The brothers test airfoils, discovering the older tables of air pressure are wrong.

1902—The brothers test their glider near Kill Devil Hills in September; They begin building a lightweight aluminum motor in December.

1903—The Wrights begin applying for a patent on their aircraft; Orville completes the world's first powered, sustained, and controlled flight, December 17.

1904—First flights of the 1904 Flyer II are made at Huffman Field.

1905—Wright Flyer III is built, the world's first practical airplane.

1906—A patent for a flying machine is awarded to the Wrights on May 23.

1908—The Wrights sign a contract with the United States Signal Corps; Patent war begins; Thomas Selfridge becomes first air crash casualty on September 17.

1909—Signal Corps officially accepts the Wright Flyer; The Wright Company is formed.

1910—First Wright Model B aircraft is built on June 29.

1911—Orville sets a world's soaring record, which lasts ten years.

1912—Wilbur dies on May 30.

1915—Wright Company is sold to a syndicate.

1917—Bishop Milton Wright dies on April 3.

1918—Orville makes his last flight.

1920—Orville is appointed a member of the National Advisory Committee for Aeronautics in January.

1928—The original 1903 Flyer is shipped to England on January 31.

1932—Wright Memorial is dedicated at Kill Devil Hills.

1942—Smithsonian Institution publishes a retraction of statements supporting Samuel Langley, ending Smithsonian-Wright feud.

1948—Orville dies on January 30; The 1903 Wright Flyer is installed in the Smithsonian on December 17.

CHAPTER NOTES

Chapter 1. Success

1. Stephen Kirk, *First in Flight, the Wright Brothers in North Carolina* (Winston-Salem, N.C.: John F. Blair, 1995), p. 313.

2. Orville Wright to Milton Wright, December 15, 1903, in Marvin W. McFarland, ed., *The Papers of Wilbur and Orville Wright* (New York: McGraw-Hill, 1952), vol. 1, p. 393.

3. Kirk, p. 182.

Chapter 2. The Bishop's Boys

1. Tom D. Crouch, *The Bishop's Boys: A Life of Wilbur and Orville Wright* (New York: W. W. Norton & Co., 1989), p. 35.

2. Orville Wright, *How We Invented the Airplane, an Illustrated History* (New York: Dover Publications, 1988), p. 11.

3. Crouch, p. 82.

4. Marvin W. McFarland, ed., *The Papers of Wilbur and Orville Wright* (New York: McGraw-Hill, 1993), vol. 1, p. 696, note 1.

Chapter 3. In Business With Bicycles

1. Wilbur Wright, April 3, 1912, in Marvin W. McFarland, ed., *The Papers of Wilbur and Orville Wright* (New York: McGraw-Hill, 1952), vol. 1, p. v.

2. Wilbur Wright, "Some Aeronautical Experiments," in McFarland, p. 103.

3. Fred Howard, *Wilbur and Orville: A Biography of the Wright Brothers* (New York: Alfred A. Knopf, 1987), p. 28.

4. Orville Wright, *How We Invented the Airplane, an Illustrated History* (New York: Dover Publications, 1988), p. 11.

5. Marvin W. McFarland, "Wilbur and Orville Wright: Seventy-Five Years After," in *The Wright Brothers: Heirs of Prometheus* (Washington, D.C.: Smithsonian Institution Press, 1978), p. 22.

6. Tom D. Crouch, *The Bishop's Boys: A Life of Wilbur and Orville Wright* (New York: W. W. Norton & Co., 1989), p. 172.

7. Orville Wright, p. 12.

8. Grover Loening, "Address at Orville Wright's 100th Birthday Anniversary, August 19th, 1971," in Ivonette Wright Miller, ed., *Wright Reminiscences* (Dayton, Ohio: The Air Force Museum Foundation, Inc., 1978), p. 78.

Chapter 4. Experiments With Gliders

1. Ivonette Wright Miller, "Speech given by Ivonette Miller at the Luncheon to Commemorate the 100th Birthday Anniversary of Orville Wright," in Ivonette Wright Miller, ed., *Wright Reminiscences* (Dayton, Ohio: The Air Force Museum Foundation, Inc., 1978), p. 72.

2. Milton Wright, "Remarks by Milton Wright, on behalf of the Estate of Orville Wright, in presenting the Kitty Hawk Aeroplane to the United States of America," in Miller, p. 68.

3. Ivonette Wright Miller, "Character Study," in Miller, p. 61.

4. Marvin W. McFarland, "Wilbur and Orville Wright: Seventy-Five Years After," in *The Wright Brothers: Heirs of Prometheus* (Washington, D.C.: Smithsonian Institution Press, 1978), pp. 22–23.

5. Stephen Kirk, *First in Flight, the Wright Brothers in North Carolina* (Winston-Salem, N.C.: John F. Blair, 1995), p. 40.

6. Fred C. Kelly, *The Wright Brothers, a Biography* (New York: Dover Publications, 1989), p. 55.

Chapter 5. Trusting Their Own Calculations

1. Fred C. Kelly, *The Wright Brothers, a Biography* (New York: Dover Publications, 1989), p. 72.

2. Ivonette Wright Miller, "Ivonette Miller's Reminiscences," in Ivonette Wright Miller, ed., *Wright Reminiscences* (Dayton, Ohio: The Air Force Museum Foundation, Inc., 1978), p. 5.

3. Fred C. Kelly, "After Kitty Hawk: a Brief Résumé," in Orville Wright, *How We Invented the Airplane, an Illustrated History* (New York: Dover Publications, 1988), p. 55.

4. Katharine Wright to her father, August 20, 1902, in Fred C. Kelly, ed., *Miracle at Kitty Hawk: The Letters of Wilbur & Orville Wright* (New York: Da Capo Press, 1996), p. 69.

5. Tom D. Crouch, *The Bishop's Boys: A Life of Wilbur and Orville Wright* (New York: W. W. Norton & Co., 1989), p. 240.

6. Roney K. Worrell, "The Wright Brothers' Pioneer Patent," *American Bar Association Journal*, October 1979, p. 1514.

7. Telegram to Bishop Milton Wright from Orville Wright, December 17, 1903.

8. Crouch, p. 271.

Chapter 6. Perfecting the Flyer

1. Fred C. Kelly, "After Kitty Hawk: a Brief Résumé," in *How We Invented the Airplane, an Illustrated History* (New York: Dover Publications, 1988), p. 51.

2. "Amos I. Root sees Wilbur Wright Fly," in *The Wright Brothers, Heirs of Prometheus* (Washington, D.C.: Smithsonian Press, 1978), p. 115.

3. Tom D. Crouch, *The Bishop's Boys: A Life of Wilbur and Orville Wright* (New York: W. W. Norton & Co., 1989), p. 292.

4. Kelly, "After Kitty Hawk: a Brief Résumé," p. 52.

5. Charles H. Gibbs-Smith, "The Wright Brothers: Their Influence," in *The Wright Brothers, Heirs of Prometheus*, p. 35.

6. Fred C. Kelly, *The Wright Brothers, a Biography Authorized by Orville Wright* (New York: Harcourt, Brace and Company, 1943), p. 193.

Chapter 7. The Wright-Curtiss Feud Begins

1. Peter M. Bowers, *Curtiss Aircraft, 1907–1947* (London: Putnam, 1979), p. 24.

2. Milton Wright, in Ivonette Wright Miller, ed., *Wright Reminiscences* (Dayton, Ohio: The Air Force Museum Foundation, Inc., 1978), p. 168.

3. Tom D. Crouch, *The Bishop's Boys: A Life of Wilbur and Orville Wright* (New York: W. W. Norton & Co., 1989), pp. 356–357.

4. Orville and Wilbur Wright, "The Wright Brothers' Aëroplane," in Orville Wright, *How We Invented the Airplane, an Illustrated History* (New York: Dover Publications, 1988), p. 81.

5. Crouch, p. 368.

6. Ibid., p. 387.

7. Orville Wright to Katharine Wright, August 27, 1908, in Fred C. Kelly, ed., *Miracle at Kitty Hawk: The Letters of Wilbur and Orville Wright* (New York: Farrar, Straus & Young, 1951), p. 298.

8. Fred Howard, *Wilbur and Orville: A Biography of the Wright Brothers* (New York: Alfred A. Knopf, 1987), p. 269.

9. Wilbur Wright to Katharine Wright, September 20, 1908, in Kelly, p. 315.

10. Horace "Bus" Wright, "Recollections," in Ivonette Wright Miller, ed., *Wright Reminiscences* (Dayton, Ohio: The Air Force Museum Foundation, Inc., 1978), p. 159.

11. Wilbur Wright to Octave Chanute, June 6, 1909, in Fred C. Kelly, ed., *Miracle at Kitty Hawk: The Letters of Wilbur and Orville Wright* (New York: Farrar, Straus & Young, 1951), p. 342.

12. Crouch, p. 402.

Chapter 8. The Patent War

1. Marvin W. McFarland, "Wilbur and Orville Wright: Seventy-Five Years After," in *The Wright Brothers, Heirs of Prometheus* (Washington, D.C.: Smithsonian Institution Press, 1978), p. 24.

2. Ibid., p. 23.

3. Roger E. Bilstein, "Popular Attitudes Towards Aviation, 1900–1925— The Airplane, the Wrights, and the American Public," in *The Wright Brothers, Heirs of Prometheus*, p. 47.

4. Tom D. Crouch, *The Bishop's Boys: A Life of Wilbur and Orville Wright* (New York: W. W. Norton & Co., 1989), p. 12.

5. Bilstein, p. 43.

Chapter 9. Life After Wilbur

1. Grover Loening, "Address at Orville Wright's 100th Birthday Anniversary, August 19th, 1971," in Ivonette Wright Miller, ed., *Wright Reminiscences* (Dayton, Ohio: The Air Force Museum Foundation, Inc., 1978), p. 80.

2. Tom D. Crouch, *The Bishop's Boys: A Life of Wilbur and Orville Wright* (New York: W. W. Norton & Co., 1989), p. 487.

3. Fred Howard, *Wilbur and Orville: A Biography of the Wright Brothers* (New York: Alfred A. Knopf, 1987), p. 404.

4. Ivonette Wright Miller in Miller, p. 18.

5. Orville Wright to C. H. Hitchcock, June 21, 1917, in Fred C. Kelly, ed., *Miracle at Kitty Hawk, The Letters of Wilbur & Orville Wright* (New York: Da Capo Press, 1996), p. 406.

6. Paul E. Garber, "Recollections and Reflections," in *The Wright Brothers: Heirs of Prometheus* (Washington, D.C.: Smithsonian Institution Press, 1978), p. 50.

7. Crouch, pp. 482–483.

8. Howard, p. 440.

Chapter 10. The Final Recognition

1. Fred C. Kelly, "Introduction," in *Orville Wright, How We Invented the Airplane, an Illustrated History* (New York: Dover Publications, 1988), p. 3.

2. Tom D. Crouch, *The Bishop's Boys: A Life of Wilbur and Orville Wright* (New York: W. W. Norton & Co., 1989), p. 529.

3. Fred C. Kelly, "After Kitty Hawk: a Brief Résumé," in *Orville Wright, How We Invented the Airplane, an Illustrated History* (New York: Dover Publications, 1988), p. 55.

4. Ibid.

GLOSSARY

derrick—An apparatus used to hoist something heavy into the air, such as an airplane.

gas-bag airship—A huge hydrogen-filled or helium-filled, football-shaped balloon with a long, narrow gondola hanging below the balloon.

gyroscope—A wheel or disk that spins around a bar mounted into a circle. As long as the wheel continues to spin rapidly, it will remain balanced on one of the ends of its bar, resisting any change in the direction of its spin.

injunction—A court order prohibiting a party from a specific course of action.

lathe—A tool that cuts material from a cylindrical piece of metal or wood by rotating it against a cutting tool.

patent—A document that grants an inventor the exclusive right to make, sell, or use the invention for a specific period of time.

pusher plane—An airplane having propellers at the rear of the wings, pushing it along.

stall—Occurs when a glider or plane stops moving forward in the air.

tractor plane—An airplane pulled by propellers at the front of the wings.

FURTHER READING

Books

Berliner, Don. Aviation: *Reaching for the Sky*. Minneapolis, Minn.: Oliver Press, 1997.

———. *Before the Wright Brothers*. Minneapolis, Minn.: Lerner Publications, 1990.

Boyne, Walter J. *The Smithsonian Book of Flight for Young People*. New York: Atheneum, 1988.

Dale, Henry. *Early Flying Machines*. New York: Oxford University Press, 1992.

Freedman, Russell. *The Wright Brothers: How They Invented the Airplane*. New York: Holiday House, 1991.

Jefferis, David. *Timelines: Flight, Fliers and Flying Machines*. New York: Franklin Watts, 1991.

Kelly, Fred C. *The Wright Brothers: A Biography*. New York: Dover Publications, 1989.

Kirk, Stephen. *First in Flight: The Wright Brothers in North Carolina*. Winston-Salem, N.C.: John F. Blair, Publisher, 1995.

Taylor, Richard L. *The First Flight: The Story of the Wright Brothers*. New York: Franklin Watts, 1990.

Young, Rosamond, and Catharine Fitzgerald. *Twelve Seconds to the Moon: A Story of the Wright Brothers*. Dayton, Ohio: United States Air Force Museum Foundation, Inc., 1983.

INDEX